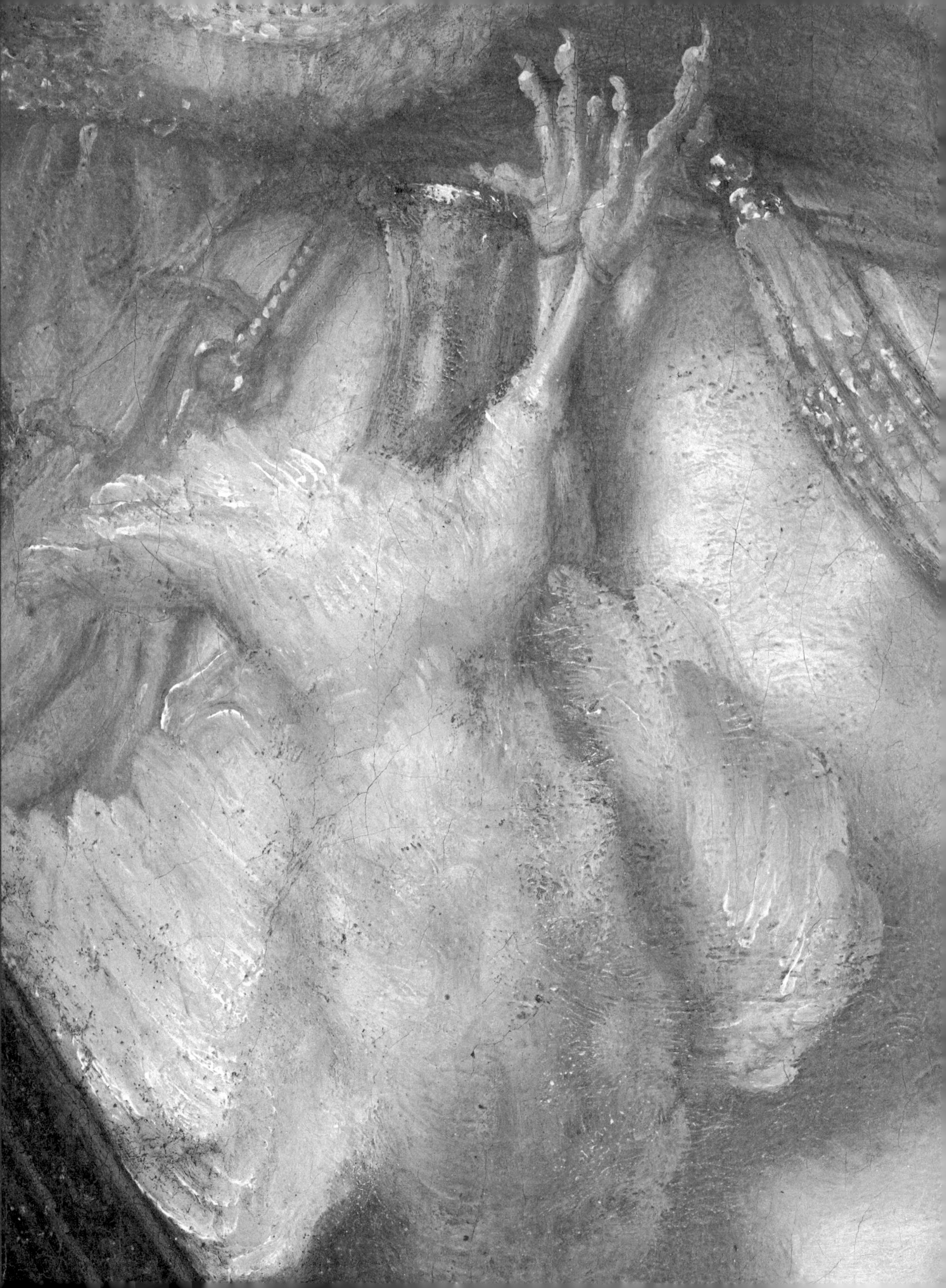

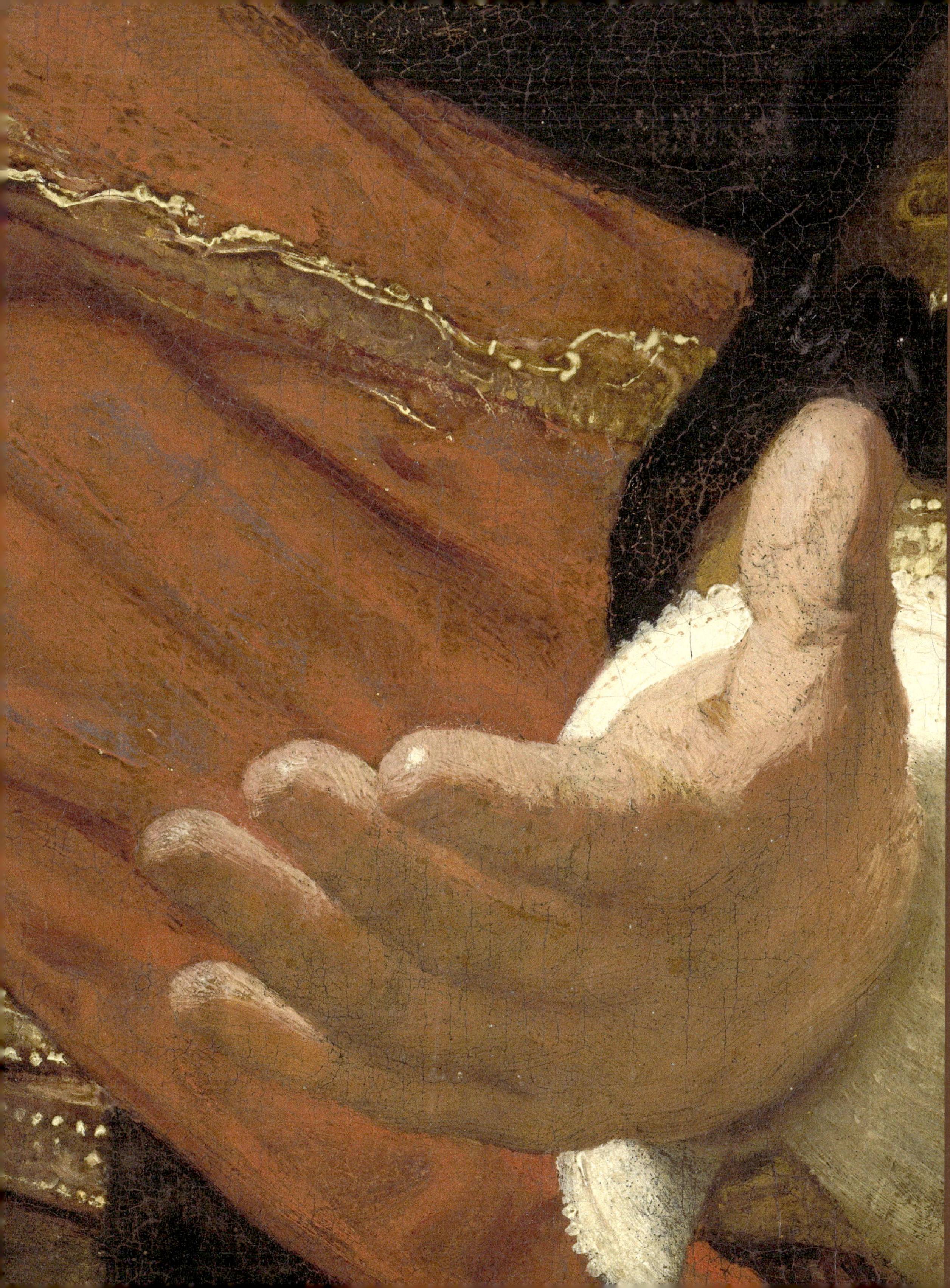

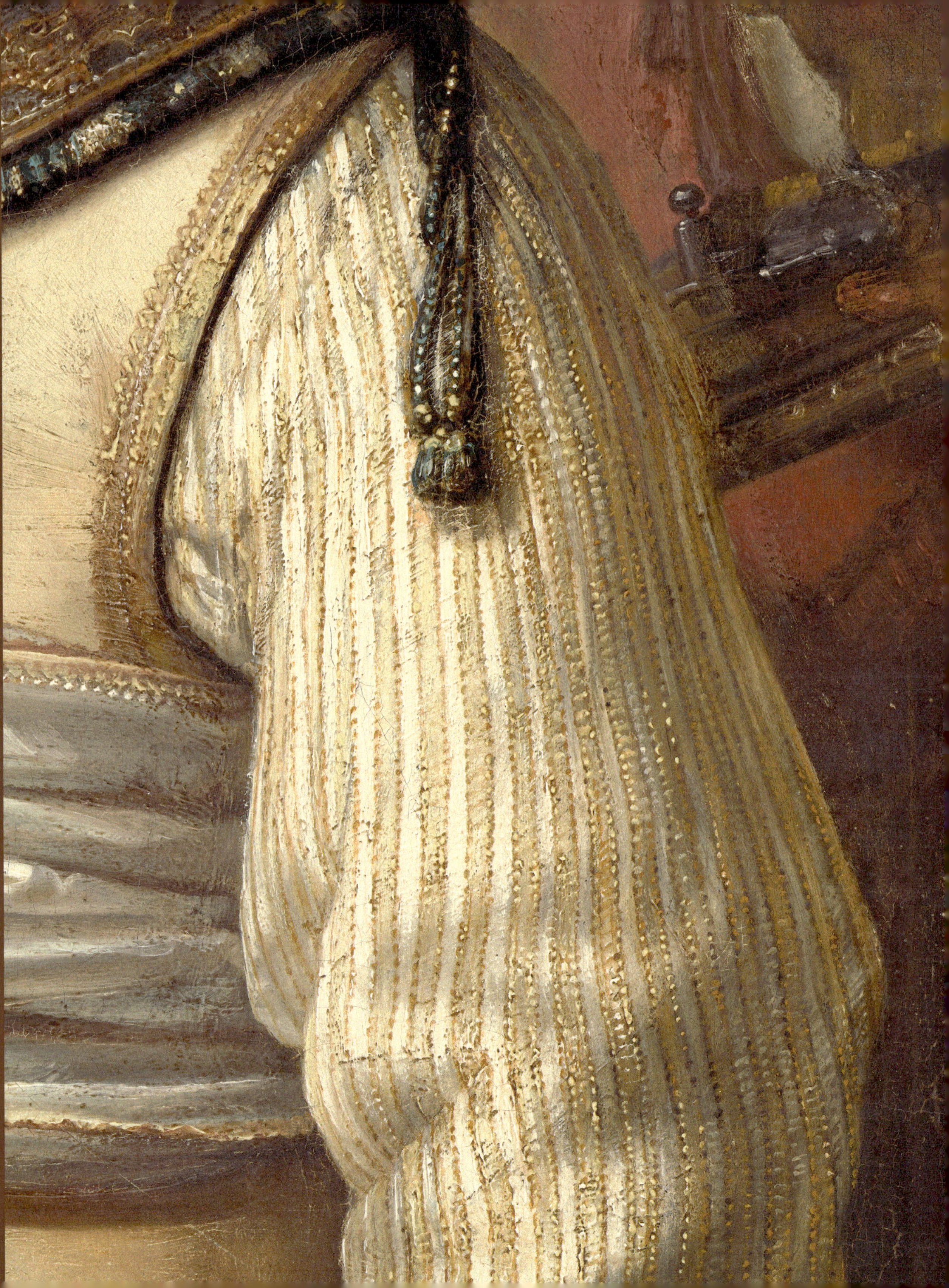

# REMBRANDT
# THE NIGHT WATCH

JONATHAN BIKKER
IN COLLABORATION WITH THE OPERATION NIGHT WATCH TEAM

RIJKS MUSEUM

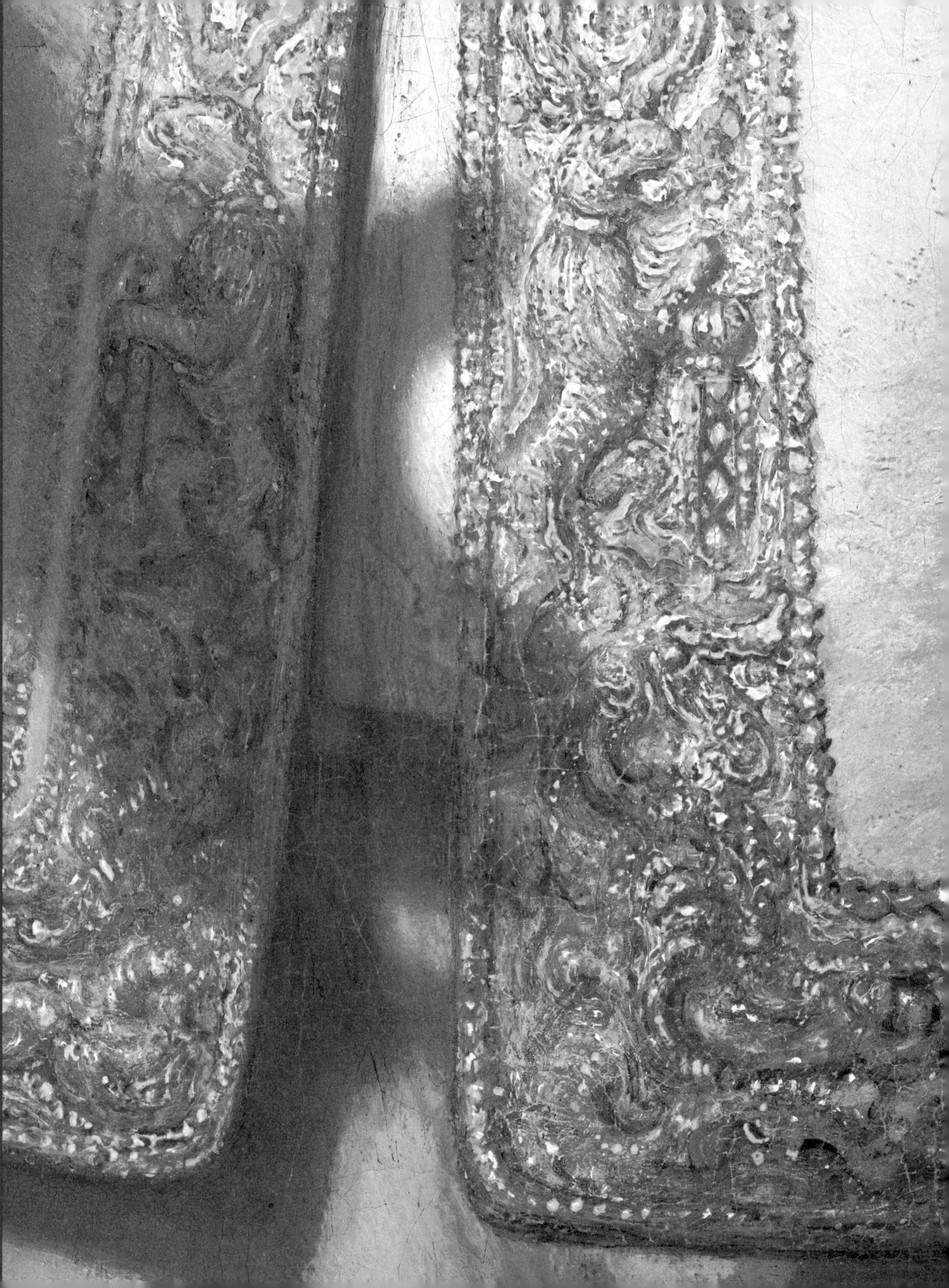

## FOREWORD

*The Night Watch* is Rembrandt's most celebrated painting and has long been the very heart of the Rijksmuseum. When the building first opened its doors in 1885, it was, in fact, designed around this monumental work. Indeed, the sheer size of the canvas and the great spectacle that unfolds on its surface make it a perfect centrepiece.

This masterpiece is the climax of the first half of Rembrandt's career, during which he established himself as the foremost Dutch artist of his generation, but it also came to signify a point of no return. Never before – and never thereafter – did he tell a story through such a complex composition, filled with action-packed figures, illuminated by incredibly subtle nuances of light and shadow. A portrait of citizens defending their beloved city Amsterdam from enemy forces during the Eighty Years' War, *The Night Watch* is the symbol par excellence of the Dutch struggle for independence. As such it is the perfect representative of the Rijksmuseum's mandate to be a place where history and art come together to tell the story of the Netherlands in all its aspects.

Always a focal point, *The Night Watch* is attracting even more attention today because of its large-scale conservation treatment, in full view of the visiting public. Operation Night Watch is the most thorough and wide-ranging research and conservation project ever carried out on Rembrandt's masterpiece. Such an enormous undertaking cannot be embarked upon without first carefully researching every aspect of the painting. Using state of the art equipment and the most advanced methods, a team of scientists, conservators, curators, photographers, documentalists and coordinators began the project in the summer of 2019. We are very grateful to the entire team that painstakingly carried out this important and fruitful research. It is with equal, if not greater, anticipation that we now follow the conservation of this national treasure.

Our sincere thanks also go to those whose generosity helped bring Operation Night Watch to life: Main Partner AkzoNobel, The Bennink Foundation, C.L. de Carvalho-Heineken, PACCAR Foundation, Piet van der Slikke & Sandra Swelheim, American Express Foundation, Familie De Rooij, Het AutoBinck Fonds, TBRM Engineering Solutions, Dina & Kjell Johnsen, Familie D. Ermia, Familie M. van Poecke, Bruker Nano Analytics, Henry M. Holterman Fonds, Irma Theodora Fonds, Luca Fonds, Piek-den Hartog Fonds, Stichting Zabawas, Cevat Fonds, Johanna Kast-Michel Fonds, Marjorie & Jeffrey A. Rosen, Stichting Thurkowfonds, Familie Van Ogtrop Fonds, FedEx Express, Airbnb, NICAS, the Night Watch Fund, the City of Amsterdam and the Amsterdam Museum.

The aim of this ambitious restoration project has always been to ensure that Rembrandt's masterpiece can be preserved and presented at its best – for the generations of today, and of the future.

Taco Dibbits
General Director, Rijksmuseum

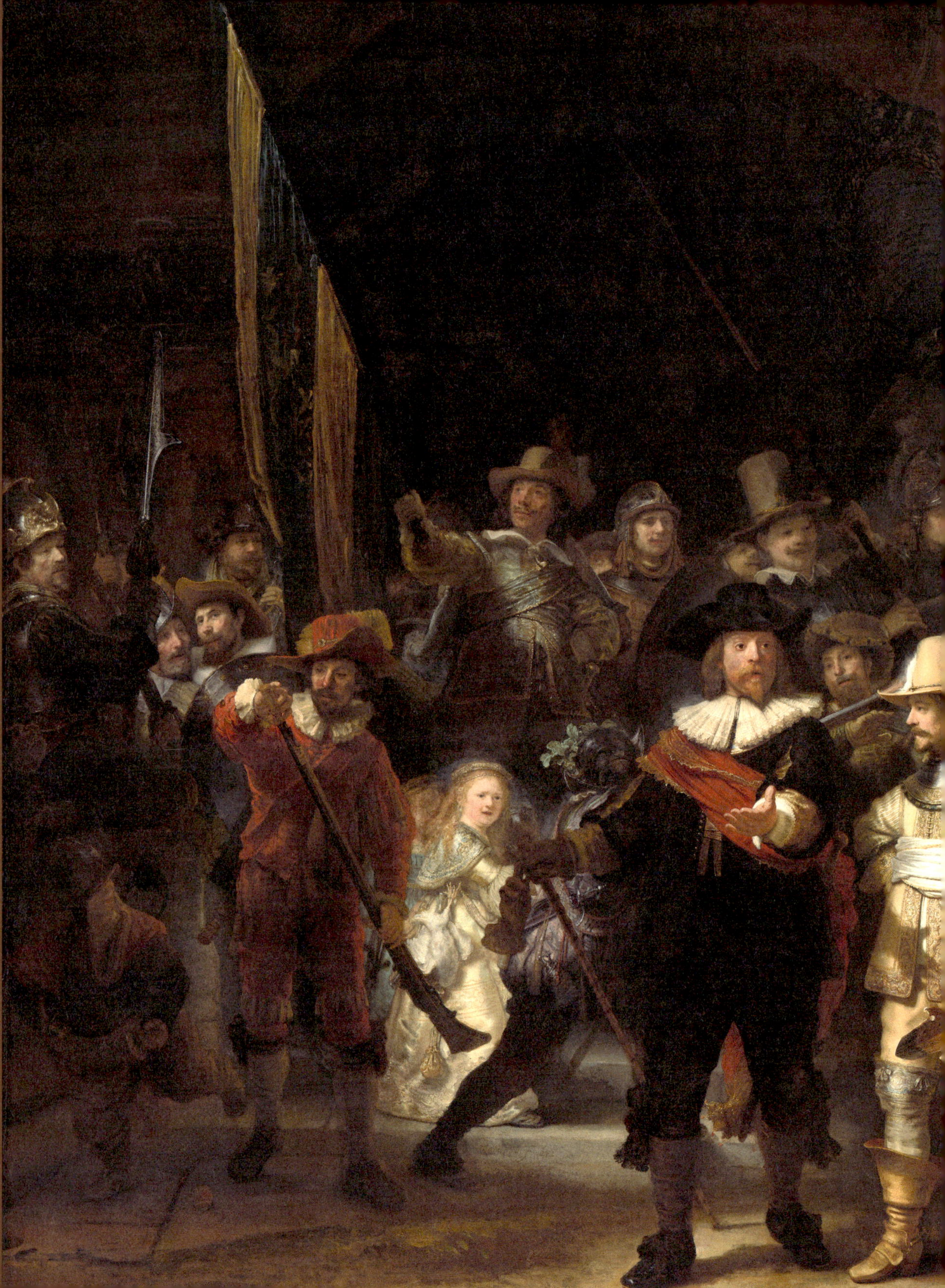

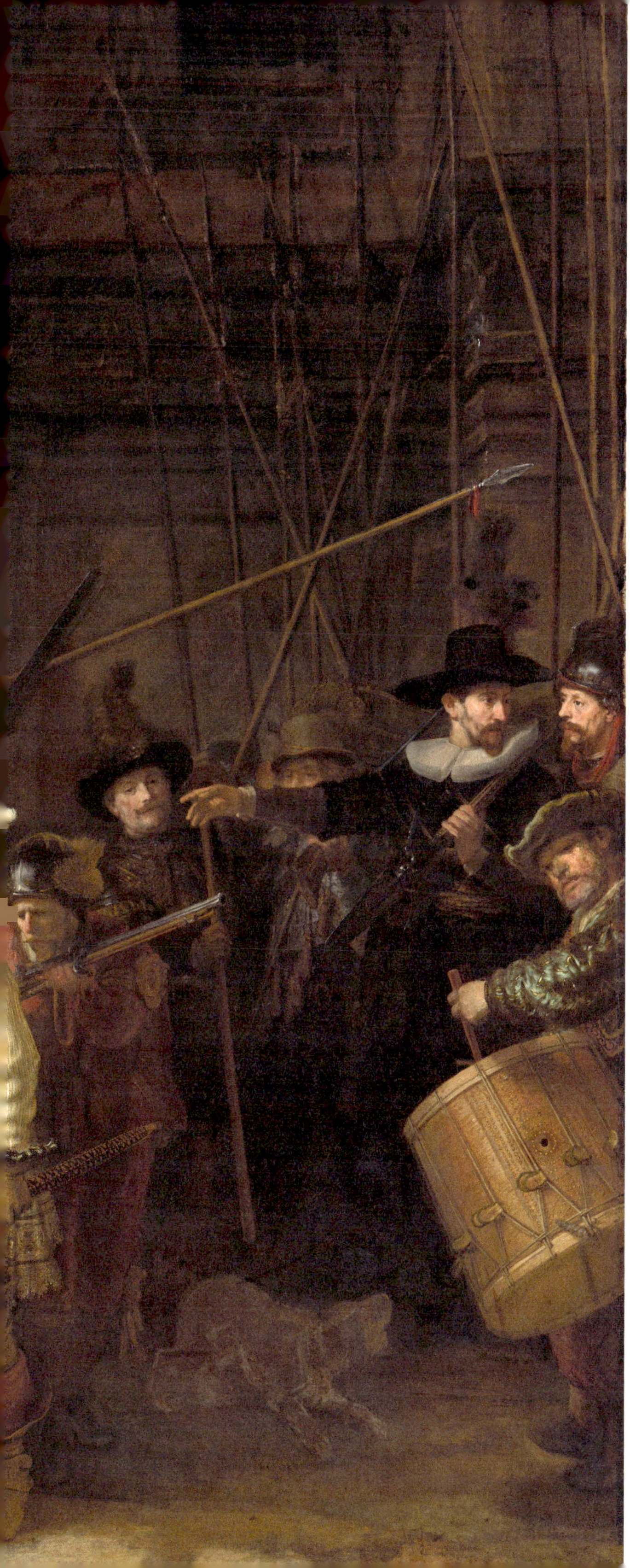

1
Rembrandt van Rijn,
*Officers and Other Civic Guardsmen of District II in Amsterdam, under the Command of Captain Frans Banninck Cocq and Lieutenant Wilhem van Ruytenburch, known as 'The Night Watch'*, 1642.
Oil on canvas, 362.5 × 436 cm (379.5 × 453.5 cm including the lining canvas).
Amsterdam, Rijksmuseum, inv. no. SK-C-5; on loan from the City of Amsterdam

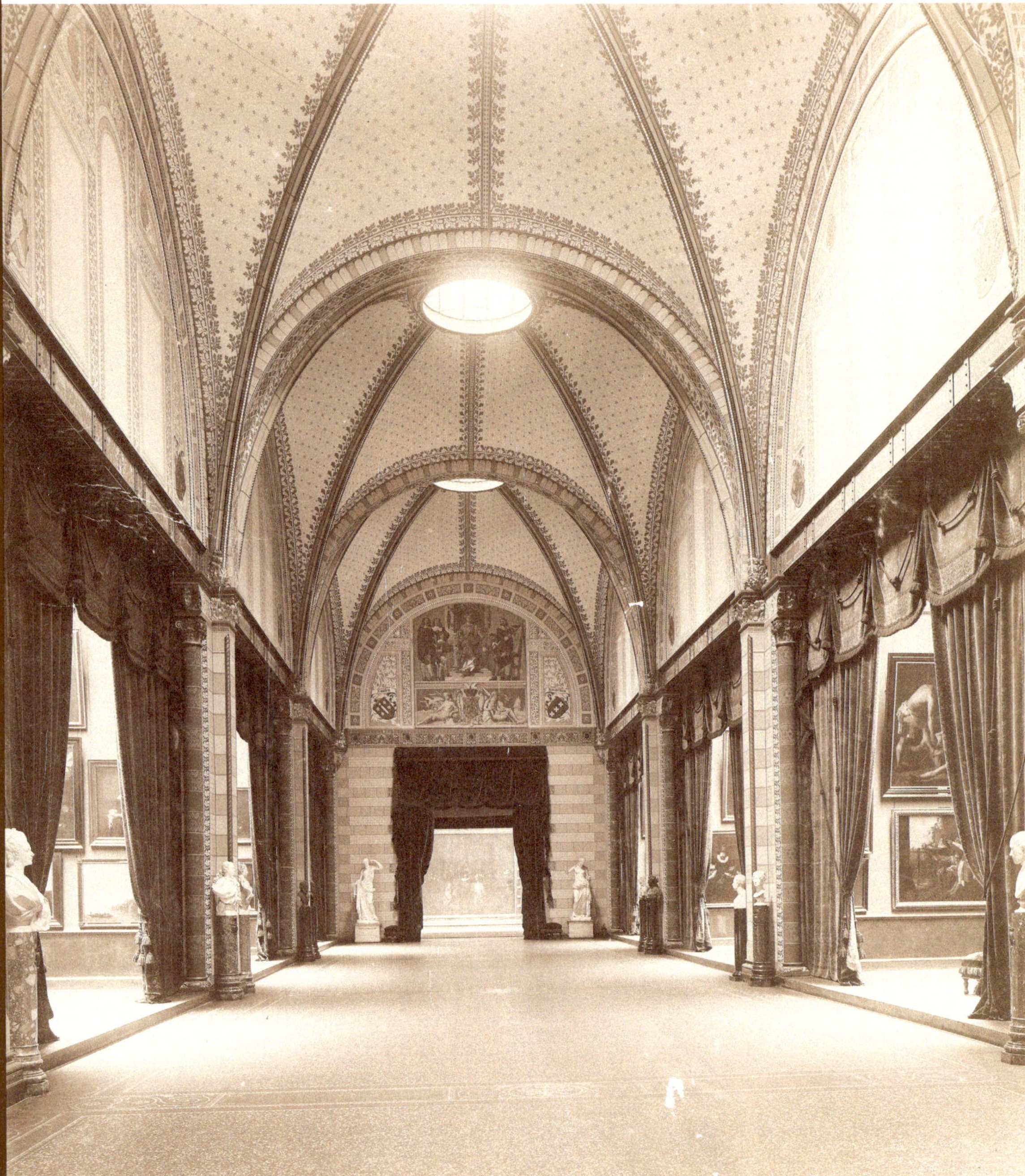

2
The Gallery of Honour of the Rijksmuseum, looking from the main hall to the Night Watch Gallery, c. 1885. Amsterdam, Rijksmuseum, inv. no. RMA-SSA-F-00047-1

## A PAINTING THAT WILL 'OUTLIVE ALL OF ITS RIVALS'

If you were asked what kind of painting *The Night Watch* [FIG. 1] is, would you say that it is a portrait? If you know the painting very well and have read about it, try to think back to the first time you saw it. What were your first impressions? The painting is, in fact, a portrait, but do not be alarmed if you did not know this, because Rembrandt and later the Rijksmuseum have deliberately gone out of their way to mislead you. Since its opening in 1885, the Rijksmuseum has most often displayed *The Night Watch* like a high altarpiece in a separate room at the end of the Gallery of Honour, a space resembling the nave of a church [FIG. 2]. Altarpieces in actual churches are never portraits, but religious scenes, often with figures performing actions that relate a story. Since the Renaissance, depictions of such biblical narratives, together with those based on classical history and mythology, have been known as 'histories', and they were long considered the most distinguished subject matter an artist could render.

As a portrait of the officers and some of the men of one of Amsterdam's civic guard companies, *The Night Watch* cannot be considered a 'history'. It should not be categorized simply as a portrait either, but, in order to be precise, it should be regarded as a corporate group portrait, which also includes pictures of board members of trade guilds and governors of charitable institutions. This was an almost exclusively Dutch type of picture and hundreds of them were made in the Republic between the second quarter of the sixteenth century and the early nineteenth century. The 'Dutchness' of the civic guard portrait in particular has often been stressed. *The Night Watch*'s subject is consequently strongly representative of seventeenth-century Dutch art, and in this respect it seems only right that it should be the centrepiece of the Rijksmuseum's collection.

Although it is strictly speaking a portrait and not a history piece, Rembrandt approached the commission as if it were a narrative from the Bible, classical history or mythology. This was already recognized in the treatise on painting written by Samuel van Hoogstraten, one of Rembrandt's former pupils, who believed it was because of this unique approach that *The Night Watch* would 'outlive all of its rivals'. Van Hoogstraten's promise of the painting's longevity would have resonated well with the portrayed guardsmen, but by the time the apprentice's book was published in 1678, the picture had already outlived them.

The primary function of all portraits is to immortalize their sitters. But in order to truly do so, a portrait has to 'live forever'. Unwittingly, this supposes that paintings, unlike mere mortals, are not subject to the ravages of time, but, instead, have been granted eternal life. Needless to say, this is a myth. While a lot of paintings have been around for a long time, they too age and are subject to such things as accidents or even vandalism. *The Night Watch* is a prime example of a picture with an eventful history. This book discusses that history, as well as what it is that makes this a work that will 'outlive all of its rivals'.

## THE AMSTERDAM CIVIC GUARD AND THEIR PORTRAITS

The civic militia as an institution had its roots in medieval times. It was organized into guilds, and in Rembrandt's day there were three *doelen* or headquarters in Amsterdam, named after the weapons – the crossbow, the longbow and the *klover* or caliver (a simple light musket) – traditionally associated with each guild. The civic guard headquarters where *The Night Watch* hung was called the Kloveniersdoelen after the last of these weapons [FIG. 12].

The Amsterdam militia was reorganized in 1580. The city was divided into districts, each with its own civic guard company under the leadership of a captain, lieutenant and ensign. At the time Rembrandt was commissioned to paint *The Night Watch* – some sixty years later – there were twenty of them. With a few exceptions, all able-bodied men between the ages of eighteen and sixty were called upon to join the company in the district where they lived on a part-time basis. Their selection was ultimately in the hands of the captain, and, over the course of the first half of the seventeenth century, the handful of clans that controlled Amsterdam city politics increasingly gained control over the selection of the captains and other officers. This nepotistic system sometimes descended into the realms of farce, as when Burgomaster Joan Munter appointed his two-year-old son Dirck to the position of ensign in 1650, and promoted him to the rank of lieutenant six years later. Service in the senior ranks of the civic guard was often a stepping stone to high office in municipal politics.

The main responsibility of the civic militia was to defend the city against attack. In the periods 1580 to 1609 and 1621 to 1648 the potential invaders were the Spanish. While Amsterdam itself was never besieged, companies of its civic guardsmen, mostly volunteers from the various districts, were sent out to assist the regular troops of the state's army at the front.

In 1529, the militia began to decorate their *doelen* with group portraits of civic guardsmen. Of the 135 surviving works, more were painted in Amsterdam – 57 to be precise – than in any other Dutch city. In 1588, Cornelis Ketel introduced an important innovation to the genre: for the first time, a company was depicted standing, life-size and full-length [FIG. 3]. This was also the first painting of the kind to reflect the new structure of the civic militia introduced in 1580. The highest-ranking officers, the captain and the lieutenant, can be identified by their weapons, and the ensign by the fact that he carries the troop's banner. The two sergeants can also be recognized by the arms they carry. Most Amsterdam civic guard portraits executed after 1588 followed Ketel's example in this regard, and *The Night Watch*, as we shall see, was no exception.

## THE BIGGEST EVER FOR JUST 1,600 GUILDERS

The earliest mention of *The Night Watch* occurs in a handwritten list of 'the public paintings preserved in the 3 doelen, as I found them on my return to Amsterdam in February 1653' compiled by the town councilman Gerard Schaep Pietersz. Rembrandt's portrait was one of seven hanging in the 'great hall' of the Kloveniersdoelen. Schaep tells us precisely where in the room each of the portraits hung [FIG. 4]. The first on his list was that of the governors of the Kloveniersdoelen [FIG. 5], which meant that it was also the most important as far as the status of the sitters was concerned. It was painted by Rembrandt's former pupil Govert Flinck in 1642 and hung above the fireplace on the short wall opposite the entrance. The other six paintings were all group portraits of civic guardsmen from the companies that used the Kloveniersdoelen as their headquarters. Between the fireplace and the windows overlooking the River Amstel hung a work by the German artist Joachim von Sandrart [FIG. 6]. Dated 1640, this was the first to be hung in the room. On the other side of the fireplace was the last portrait made for the great hall [FIG. 7]. This work of 1645 was also painted by Flinck, the only artist to receive two commissions.

Three monumental canvases, all dating from 1642, hung on the long wall facing the windows. One of them was *The Night Watch*, but it did not have pride of place in the centre. That spot was reserved for the portrait by Nicolaes Eliasz Pickenoy, which today is widely regarded as the most boring of the entire ensemble [FIG. 8]. Flanking Pickenoy's painting on the left was *The Night Watch*, and on the right a militia piece by Jacob Backer [FIG. 9]. It should be pointed out that the position of *The Night Watch* in the corner of the room was not a slight to Rembrandt. The company in Pickenoy's painting would have been given centre stage because its captain, Jan Claesz van Vlooswijck, had held that post much longer than those in Rembrandt's and Backer's portraits. Van Vlooswijck, moreover, was also one of the governors of the Kloveniersdoelen. The canvases on the long wall of the great hall were the largest civic guard portraits ever executed, and possibly the largest paintings in Amsterdam at the time. All three were subsequently cut down, Backer's less so than the others. While a few of the militia pieces made earlier for the other *doelen* were wider, those by Rembrandt, Pickenoy and Backer were a metre or more taller than their nearest competitors. A year later, in 1643, when Bartholomeus van der Helst's more than 7-metre-wide canvas was installed above the large fireplace on the entrance wall [FIG. 10], the Kloveniersdoelen could also claim the widest civic guard portrait in Amsterdam. The enormous dimensions of the paintings meant that all the figures could be full-length and more than life-size, which was the case nowhere else in the Amsterdam *doelen*.

Within a mere five years, all the walls of the great hall of the Kloveniersdoelen were filled with paintings. Various theories have been put forward to account for this enormous undertaking. In the earliest dated portrait, the one by Von Sandrart, the men are gathered around a sculpted bust of Maria de' Medici, the widow of King Henry IV of France. A poem by Joost van den Vondel, once visible on the piece of paper beneath it, informs us that they have come together in anticipation of her arrival in Amsterdam on 1 September 1638. Exiled from France by her son and irredeemably broke, Maria de' Medici was not the most glamorous or politically important royal, but the city nevertheless turned her five-day visit into the most impressive public ceremony Amsterdam had ever seen. As part of the show, all four thousand members of the civic guard, decked out in their finest military outfits and carrying their weapons,

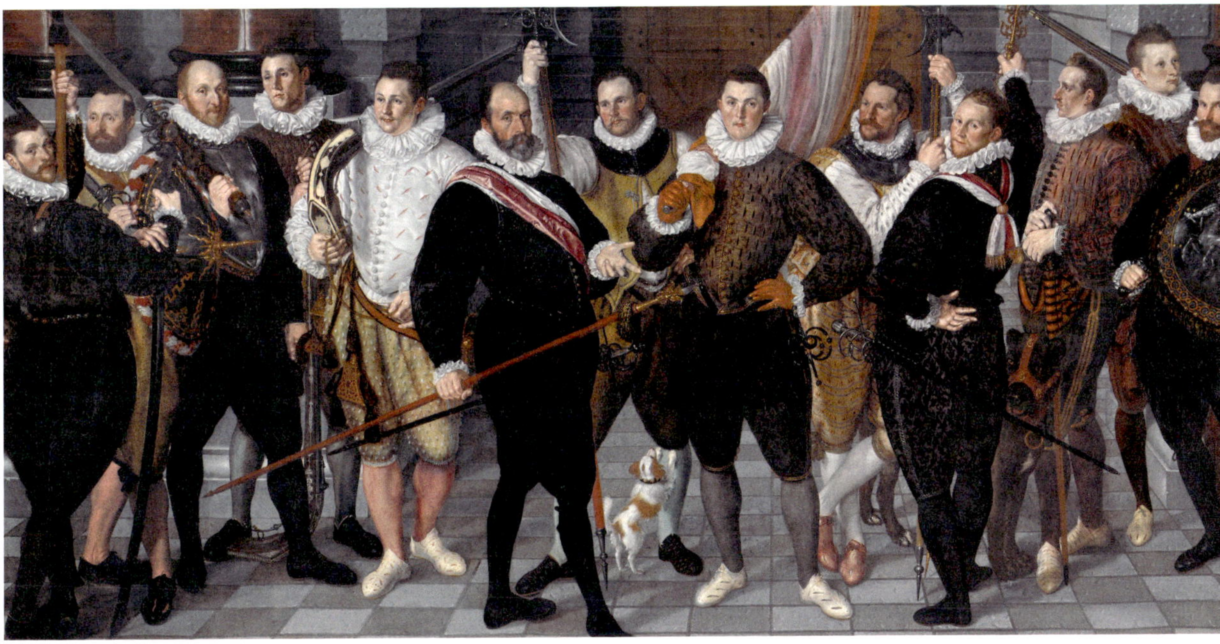

3
Cornelis Ketel, *Officers and Other Civic Guardsmen of District I in Amsterdam, under the Command of Captain Dirck Jacobsz Rosecrans and Lieutenant Pauw*, 1588.
Oil on canvas, 208 × 410 cm.
Amsterdam, Rijksmuseum, inv. no. SK-C-378; on loan from the City of Amsterdam

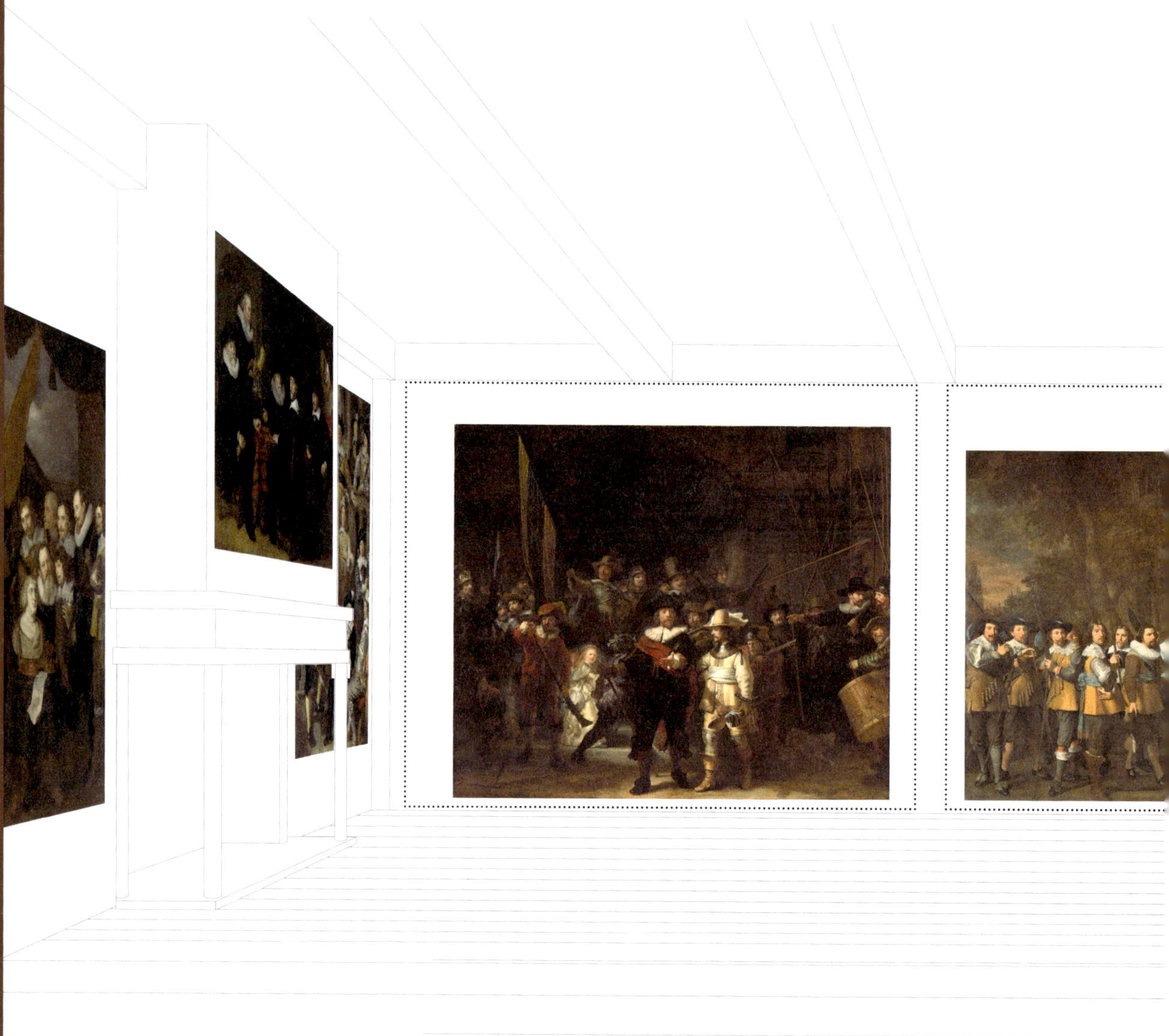

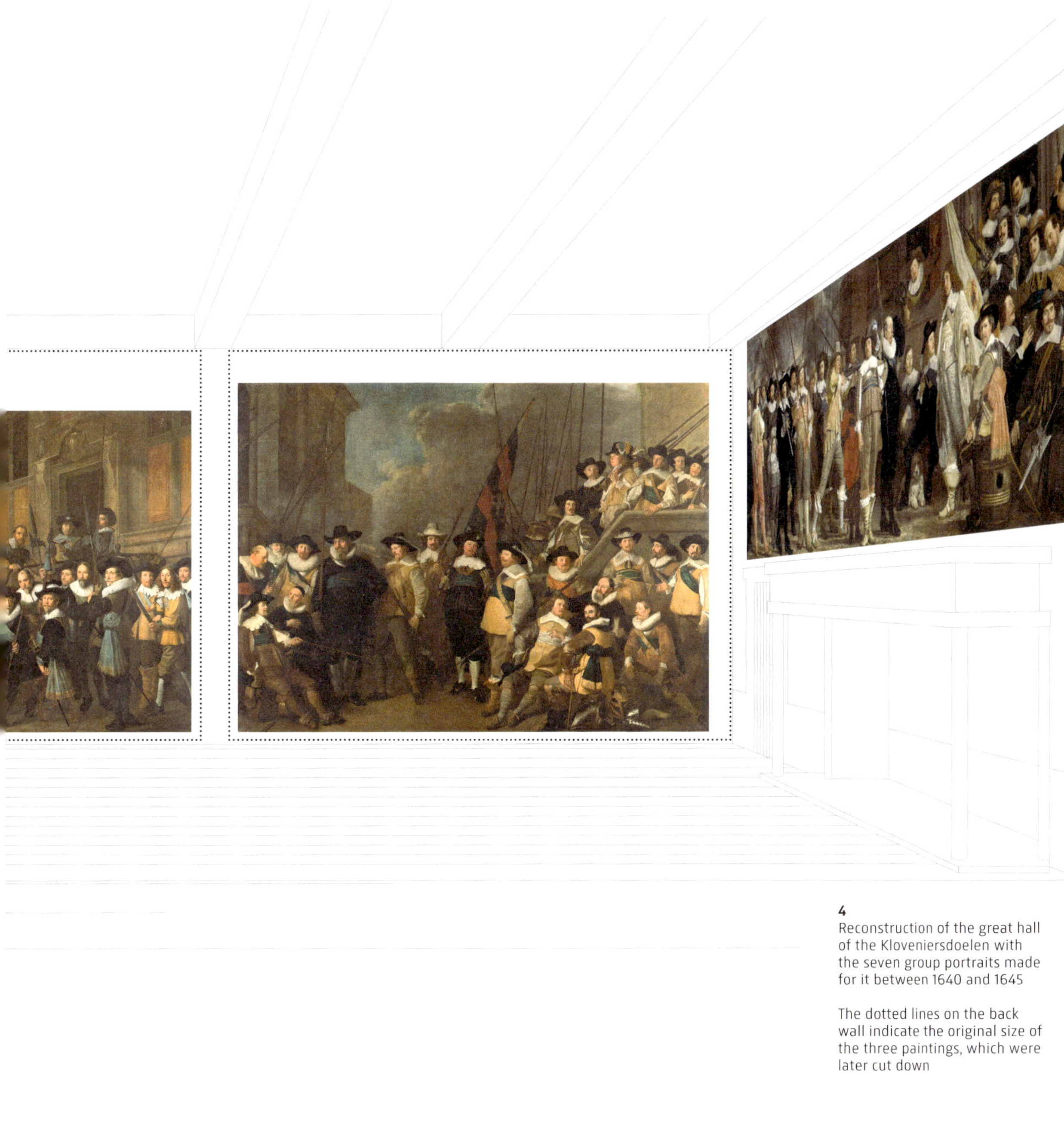

4
Reconstruction of the great hall of the Kloveniersdoelen with the seven group portraits made for it between 1640 and 1645

The dotted lines on the back wall indicate the original size of the three paintings, which were later cut down

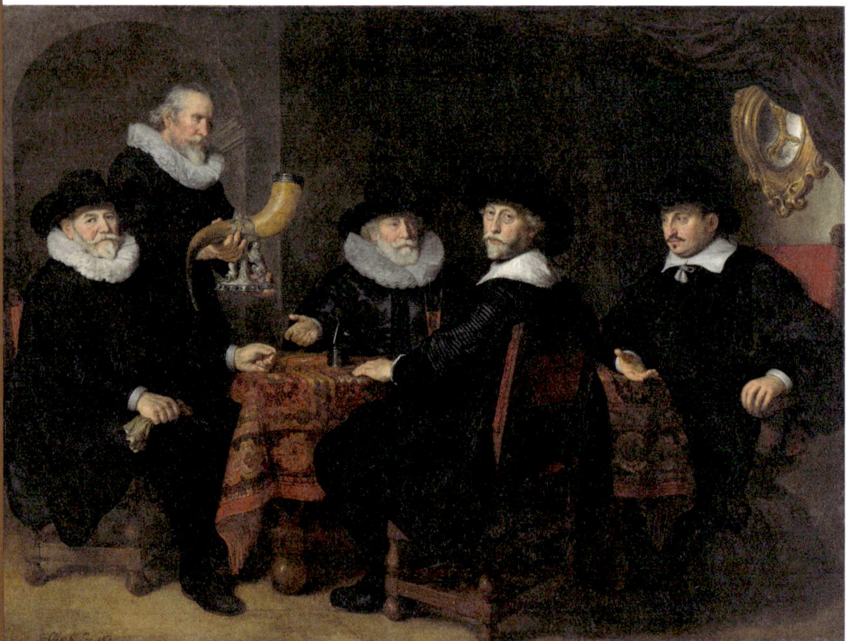

**5**
Govert Flinck, *Portrait of the Governors of the Kloveniersdoelen*, 1642. Oil on canvas, 203 × 278 cm. Amsterdam, Rijksmuseum, inv. no. SK-C-370; on loan from the City of Amsterdam

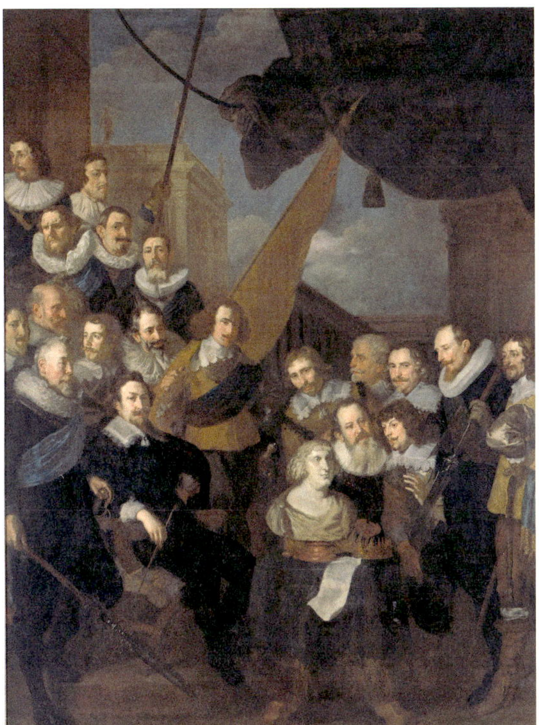

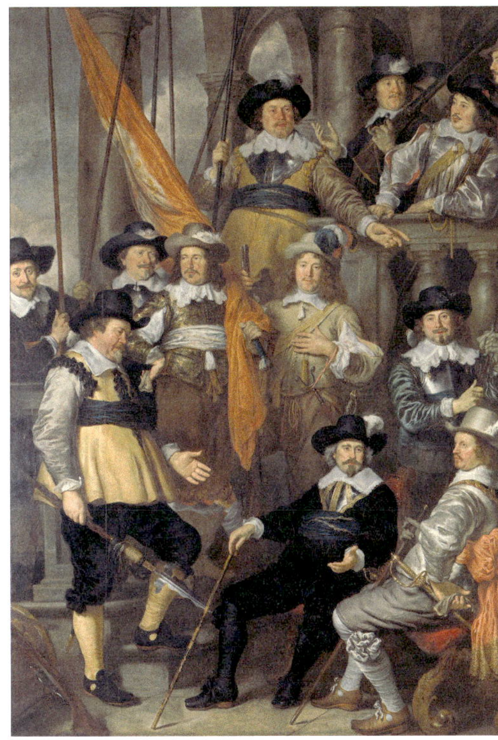

**6**
Joachim von Sandrart, *Officers and Other Civic Guardsmen of District XIX in Amsterdam, under the Command of Captain Cornelis Bicker and Lieutenant Frederick van Banchem, Waiting to Welcome Maria de' Medici, 1 September 1638*, 1640. Oil on canvas, 343 × 258 cm. Amsterdam, Rijksmuseum, inv. no. SK-C-393; on loan from the City of Amsterdam

**7**
Govert Flinck, *Officers and Other Civic Guardsmen of District XVIII in Amsterdam, under the Command of Captain Albert Bas and Lieutenant Lucas Pietersz Conijn*, 1645. Oil on canvas, 347 × 244 cm. Amsterdam, Rijksmuseum, inv. no. SK-C-371; on loan from the City of Amsterdam

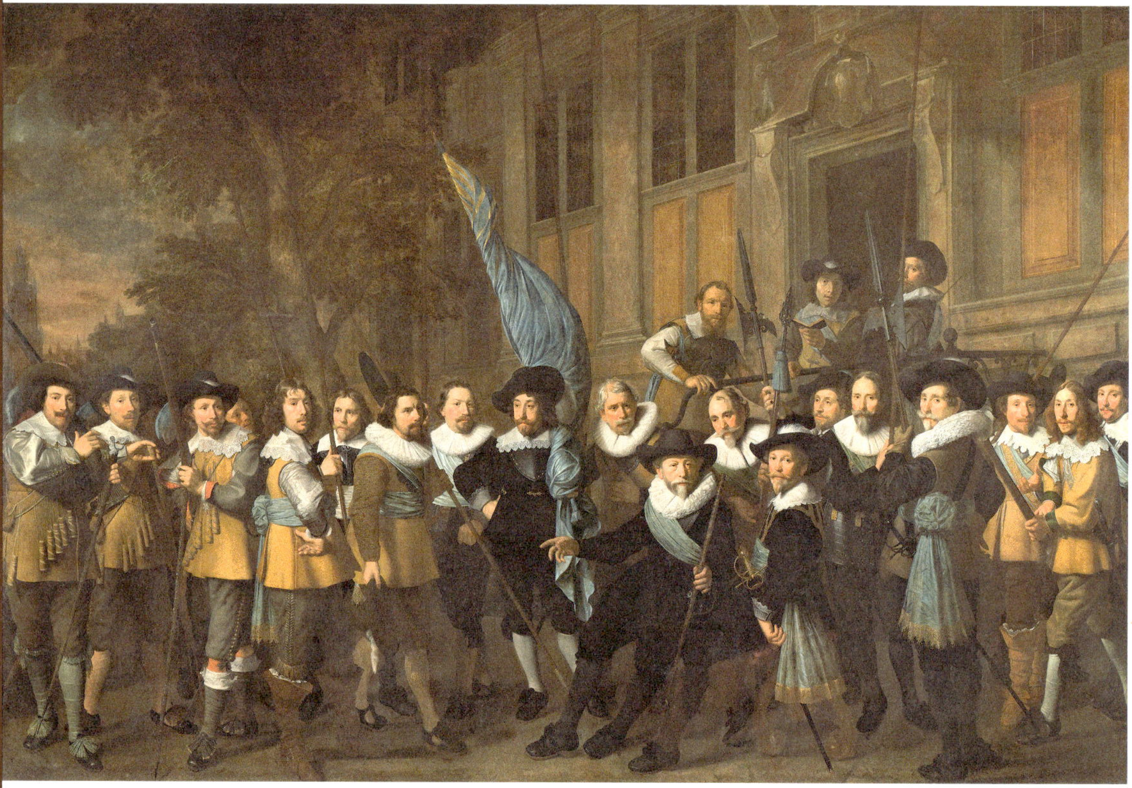

**8**
Nicolaes Eliasz Pickenoy,
*Officers and Other Civic Guardsmen of District IV in Amsterdam, under the Command of Captain Jan Claesz van Vlooswijck and Lieutenant Gerrit Hudde*, 1642.
Oil on canvas, 340 × 527 cm.
Amsterdam, Rijksmuseum,
inv. no. SK-C-1177; on loan from the City of Amsterdam

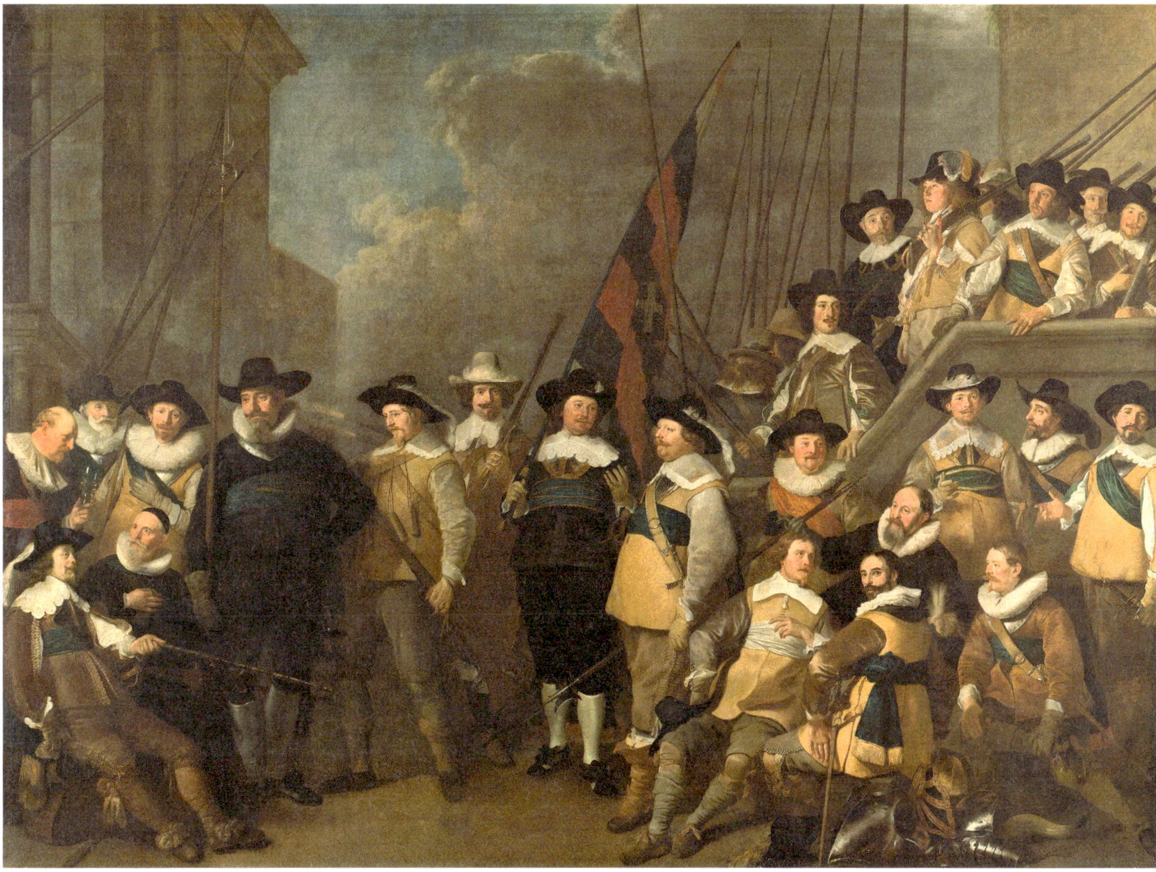

**9**
Jacob Backer, *Officers and Other Civic Guardsmen of District V in Amsterdam, under the Command of Captain Cornelis de Graeff and Lieutenant Hendrick Lauwrensz*, 1642. Oil on canvas, 367 × 511 cm. Amsterdam, Rijksmuseum, inv. no. SK-C-1174; on loan from the City of Amsterdam

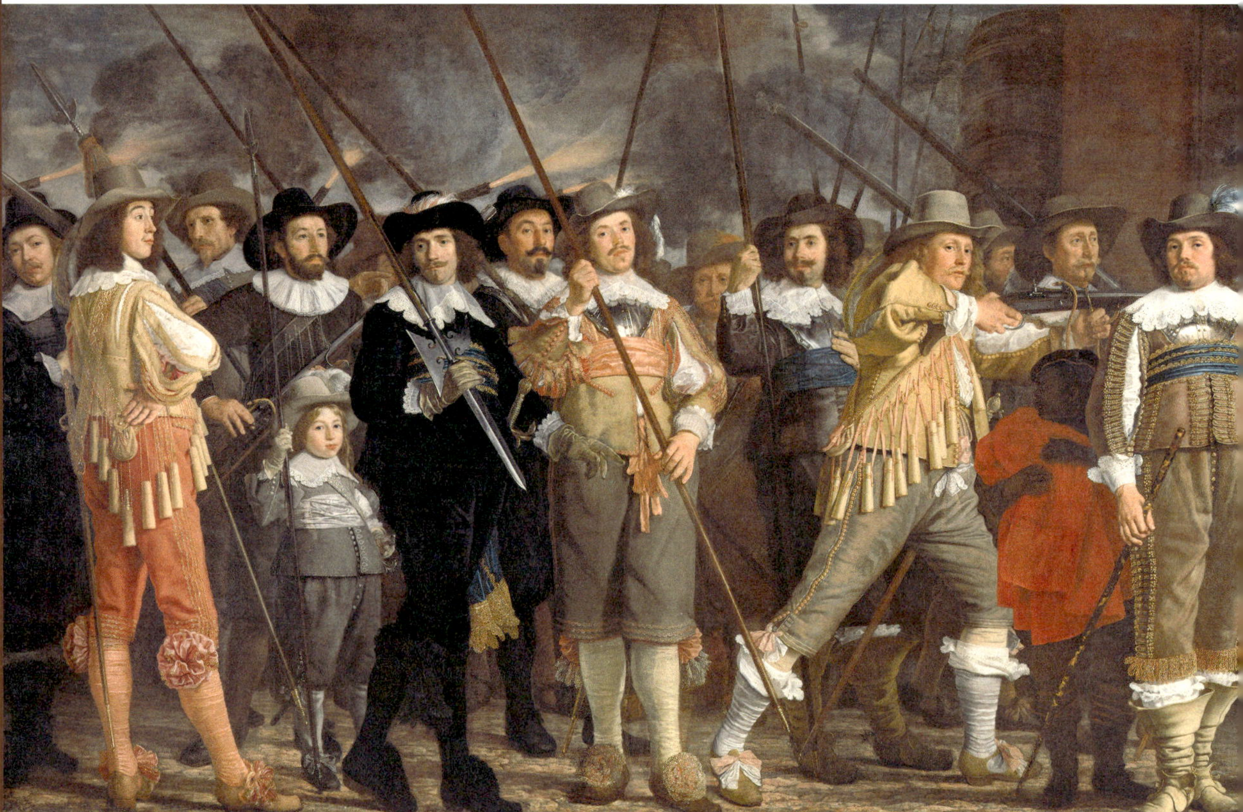

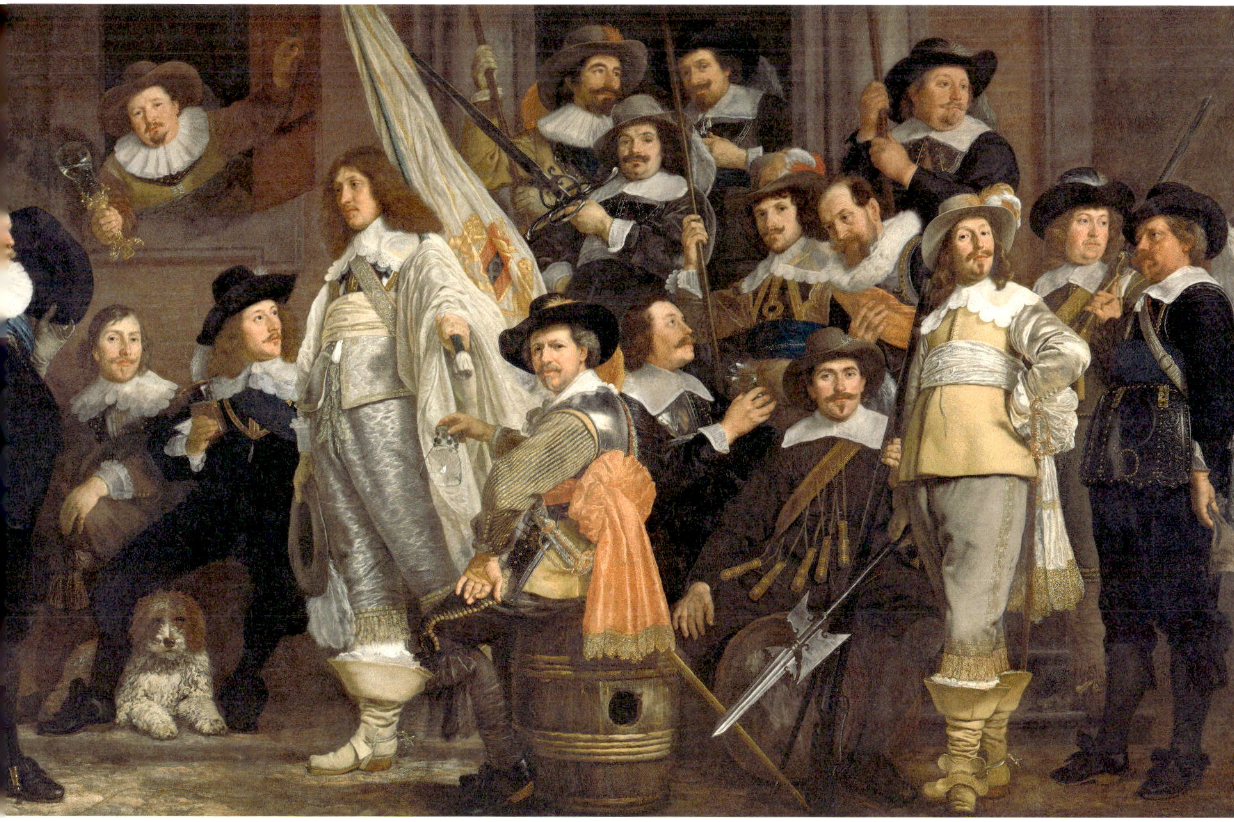

**10**
Bartholomeus van der Helst, *Officers and Other Civic Guardsmen of District VIII of Amsterdam, under the Command of Captain Roelof Bicker and Lieutenant Jan Michielsz Blaeuw*, 1643. Oil on canvas, 235 × 750 cm.
Amsterdam, Rijksmuseum, inv. no. SK-C-375; on loan from the City of Amsterdam

were in attendance [FIG. 11]. However, the notion that the other five portraits in the great hall also depict companies of guardsmen participating in the ceremonies does not hold water. The officers in some of the paintings did not occupy those posts in September 1638. Frans Banninck Cocq, for example, was the lieutenant of a different district at the time, not the captain of district II, the one represented in Rembrandt's painting.

The great hall was located on the second floor of a magnificent seventeenth-century extension to the medieval tower, called Swygh Utrecht, that had served as the headquarters of the Kloveniers since 1522 [FIG. 12]. With its 4-metre-high ceilings and generous floor plan, it was an imposing space, designed to impress, very unlike the dark, cramped reception rooms of the other two *doelen*. The civic guardsmen were not the only ones to use it; the city government, for example, held its annual banquets there. The hall itself must have been regarded as something of an attraction, for it was shown to important visitors to the city. Was it the completion of the extension housing the great hall that prompted the commissioning of the seven portraits? This seductively simple explanation does not work either, because it has been established recently that the extension was finished in 1630.

Despite the various dates of the seven portraits, some scholars have argued that rather than coming together in a piecemeal fashion over time as they had in the other Amsterdam civic guard headquarters, the decorations of the great hall followed a predetermined plan. Among the arguments put forward for this theory is the contention that the six militia pieces filled the walls of the hall from floor to ceiling. Subsequently, however, it was demonstrated that this was definitely not the case for the south-east wall, where the civic guard portraits by Von Sandrart and Flinck hung. Another argument, that the painting by Von Sandrart originally hung elsewhere but was moved to the Kloveniersdoelen and radically altered in format in order to fit into the ensemble, has also been disproved. Instead, that painting had undoubtedly been ordered as an independent work celebrating the company's role in the festivities for Maria de' Medici's visit. Because the long wall had a series of small windows at the time, it was hung to the left of the fireplace on the short wall opposite the entrance, which was then the best available spot. The hanging of Von Sandrart's painting in 1640 probably prompted the captains of three of the other companies associated with the Kloveniersdoelen and its governors to have their portraits made as well.

We know the exact date of delivery for one of the portraits that was finished in 1642 because of a very unusual wager made by Bartholomeus van der Helst and one of the men portrayed in Pickenoy's painting, an apothecary by the name of Pieter Herbers. Pickenoy's slowness was legendary, and his erstwhile pupil Van der Helst bet Herbers that he would not be able to complete his civic guard piece by the deadline of 28 July 1642. It turned out that this time around Pickenoy was actually ahead of schedule; his painting was installed on 16 July 1642. If Rembrandt had to deliver *The Night Watch* on or around the same date, he would have had a hard time of it, as his wife Saskia Uylenburgh died a little more than a month earlier on 14 June 1642. Although the exact date of delivery for *The Night Watch* cannot be established, we do know that Rembrandt would have had more than a year to work on it. A shield with the names of the civic guardsmen portrayed in it was added to the painting sometime between 1642 and 1655 by another artist [FIG. 15]. Among them is that of Jan Claesz Leijdeckers, who was buried on 27 December 1640, which means that Rembrandt must have received the commission before that date.

A contemporary of Rembrandt's, Hans Bontemantel, informs us in the notes he made on his city and its institutions that the militia pieces were financed by the civic guardsmen themselves. In the case of *The Night Watch* this is confirmed by statements made by two of the sitters in 1658, which also tell us how much they paid. One of them simply said that 'the painting cost the sum of sixteen hundred guilders', while the other was more specific: 'he was painted and portrayed by Rembrandt van Rijn, art painter, with other persons of their company and corporalship, sixteen of them, in a painting now standing in the great hall of the Kloveniersdoelen and that each of them, as far as he the witness remembers, paid for being painted the sum of one hundred guilders on average, one paying more and the other less, depending on their place in it'. According to this guardsman, there were only sixteen people portrayed in *The Night Watch*, whereas there are eighteen names recorded on the shield that was added later on. He may not have counted the captain and lieutenant among the sitters, and they perhaps paid significantly more than the lower-ranking officers and regular guardsmen.

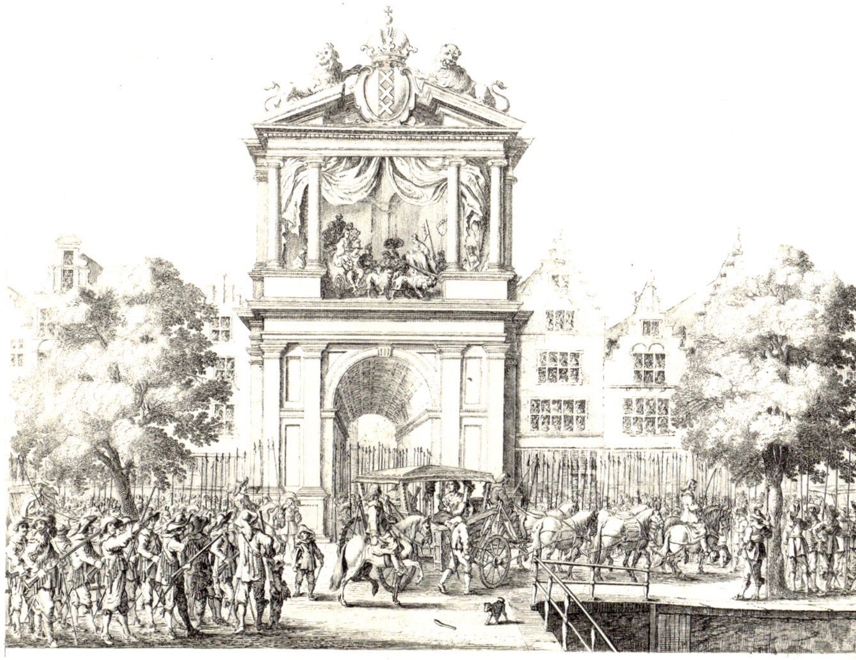

**11**
Salomon Savery after Jan Martsen the Younger, *Joyous Entry of Maria de' Medici at the Oudezijds Voorburgwal in front of the Hoogstraat*, 1638. Engraving, 297 × 388 mm. Amsterdam, Rijksmuseum, inv. no. RP-P-OB-76.459

Musketeers and their powder boys line the street in the foreground of this print. The pikemen form two orderly rows in front of the arch on the left and in the background

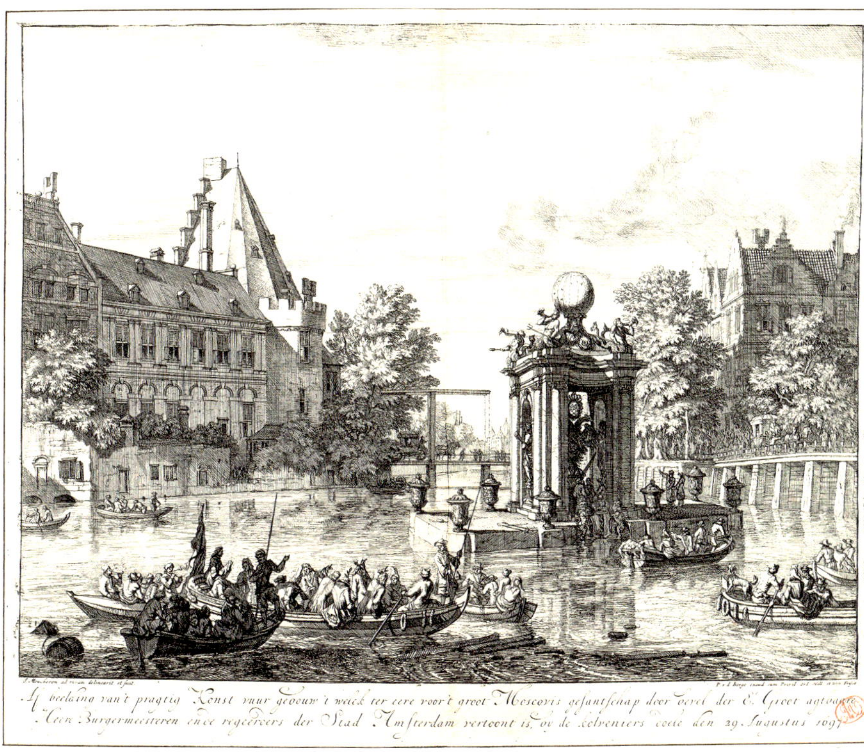

**12**
Isaac de Moucheron, *Firework Island in the River Amstel on the Occasion of the Visit of the Muscovite Ambassadors, with the Kloveniersdoelen Buildings in the Background* (on the left), 1697. Etching, 378 × 460 mm. Amsterdam, Rijksmuseum, inv. no. RP-P-AO-28-55

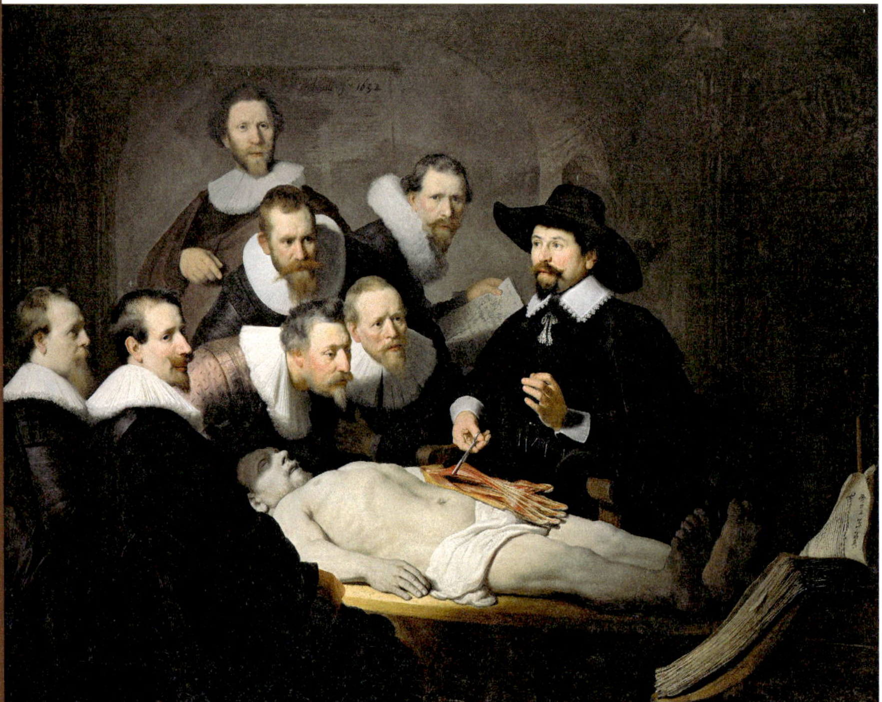

**13**
Rembrandt van Rijn,
*The Anatomy Lesson of Dr Nicolaes Tulp*, 1632.
Oil on canvas, 169.5 × 216.5 cm.
The Hague, Royal Cabinet of Paintings Mauritshuis, inv. no. 146

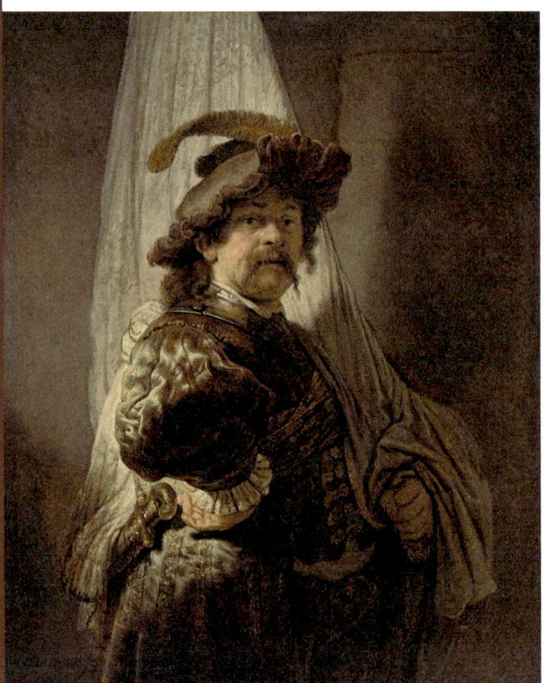

**14**
Rembrandt van Rijn, *The Standard-Bearer*, 1636. Oil on canvas, 102.6 × 97.5 cm. Amsterdam, Rijksmuseum, inv. no. SK-A-5092; purchased by the Dutch State with the support of the members of the Rembrandt Association (thanks in part to its Stortenbeker Fonds, A.M. Roeters van Lennep Fonds, Nationaal Fonds Kunstbezit, Nationaal Fonds 1930, Acquoy-Nairac Fonds, Mevrouw dr. E. Frederiks Fonds, Mevrouw J.J. den Boer-den Herder Fonds, Cleyndert Fonds, Van Rijn Fonds, Saskia Fonds, Fonds voor Klassieke Beeldende Kunst, Themafonds 17de-eeuwse schilderkunst, Warning-Meijaard Fonds, Daan Cevat Fonds, the annual contribution of the Prins Bernhard Cultuurfonds and additional donations from members), the Rijksmuseum Fonds (Hans & Hedy de Klerk, Conrad Whelan 42 Fund, Anita Nijboer Fonds, the International Circle and other private donors) and The Friends Lottery.

In 1686, the Italian writer Filippo Baldinucci, whose informant was Bernard Keil, a pupil of Rembrandt's in the early 1640s, recorded a much higher sum for the entire composition: 4,000 guilders. Whatever the case may be, 1,600 guilders for *The Night Watch* seems a pittance when compared to the 500 guilders Rembrandt charged one of his patrons around this time for a standing, full-length portrait. On the other hand, 100 guilders a head is 40 guilders more than Rembrandt's colleagues Thomas de Keyser and Frans Hals had agreed to be paid by the guardsmen they portrayed in 1632 and 1637 respectively.

## WHY REMBRANDT?

It may seem an odd question, but it is one worth asking. The other two artists whose paintings came to decorate the long wall of the great hall in 1642 already had one civic guard piece, in the case of Jacob Backer, and three pieces, in the case of Nicolaes Eliasz Pickenoy, under their belts. *The Night Watch* is Rembrandt's first and only militia portrait. By 1640, however, he was at the height of his career. An Englishman who travelled through the Netherlands in that year noted in his journal: 'As for the art off Painting and the affection off the people to Pictures, I thincke none other goe beeyond them, there having bin in this Country Many excellent Men in thatt Faculty, some att Presentt, as Rimbrantt.' Rembrandt's significant reputation was also remarked upon by Jan Jansz Orlers in his 1641 description of the artist's birthplace, Leiden: 'He was so talented that he has since become one of the most esteemed painters of this century'. Additionally, Orlers informs us that Rembrandt moved to Amsterdam from Leiden 'because his work and art had greatly pleased and impressed the citizens and residents of Amsterdam, and because he received frequent portrait commissions, as well as requests for other pictures'.

During the course of the 1630s, Rembrandt had in fact become the most sought-after portraitist in Amsterdam. While he had as yet to tackle the subject of the civic guard, he had already painted a group portrait, *The Anatomy Lesson of Dr Nicolaes Tulp*, in 1632 [FIG. 13]. Based on this work alone, the commissioners of *The Night Watch* would have been able to anticipate that in making their picture Rembrandt would go far beyond the confines of the standard group portrait. A few years later, the artist executed a work that probably served as a kind of advertisement for securing a commission for a militia piece. In 1635, he had moved to Nieuwe Doelenstraat, which was practically next door to the Kloveniersdoelen. In 1636, he painted *The Standard-Bearer* [FIG. 14], which already displays a number of the innovative features of *The Night Watch*, such as a dynamic composition, the use of sixteenth-century clothing and phenomenal light/dark contrasts.

Some of the other artists who worked on the decorations of the great hall were already well known to the companies they portrayed. Von Sandrart, for example, lived across the canal from Captain Cornelis Bicker's brother Jan and had painted portraits of two of his nephews and their wives in 1639. Bartholomeus van der Helst and most likely Jacob Backer as well lived in the districts of the companies they portrayed. Rembrandt did not live in district II, and nor did he have, as far as we know, any connection to Frans Banninck Cocq. He did, though, have a link with the captain's predecessor, Pieter Reael, who as one of the governors of the Kloveniersdoelen may have played a role in organizing the decoration of the great hall. Reael's favourite nephew, Joannes Wtenbogaert, was portrayed by Rembrandt in an etching in 1639. The artist also knew one of the regular guardsmen he pictured, Jan Claesz Leijdeckers (no. 24), whose nephew, the painter Gerbrand van den Eeckhout, probably trained with the master in the late 1630s and was later described as his 'great friend'.

## THIRTY-FOUR FIGURES, BUT ONLY EIGHTEEN GUARDSMEN

In 1715 *The Night Watch* was transferred to Amsterdam's city hall, the present-day Royal Palace on Dam Square, where it was cut down on all sides to fit between two doors. The left side of Rembrandt's painting, where three figures were removed, suffered the most. A contemporary copy gives us an idea of how it originally looked [FIG. 16].

The shield later added to *The Night Watch* carries the names of eighteen militiamen, but there were thirty-four figures in all in the original painting. This use of 'extras', especially their number and the fact they are integrated with the guardsmen, is one of the things that sets Rembrandt's painting apart from all other civic guard portraits. Cornelis Ketel's 1588 group portrait [FIG. 3] can serve as an example of the usual strategy in which only members of the company in question were shown. Some of the other portraits in the great hall, such as Backer's, include a few extras, but they occupy inconspicuous positions in the

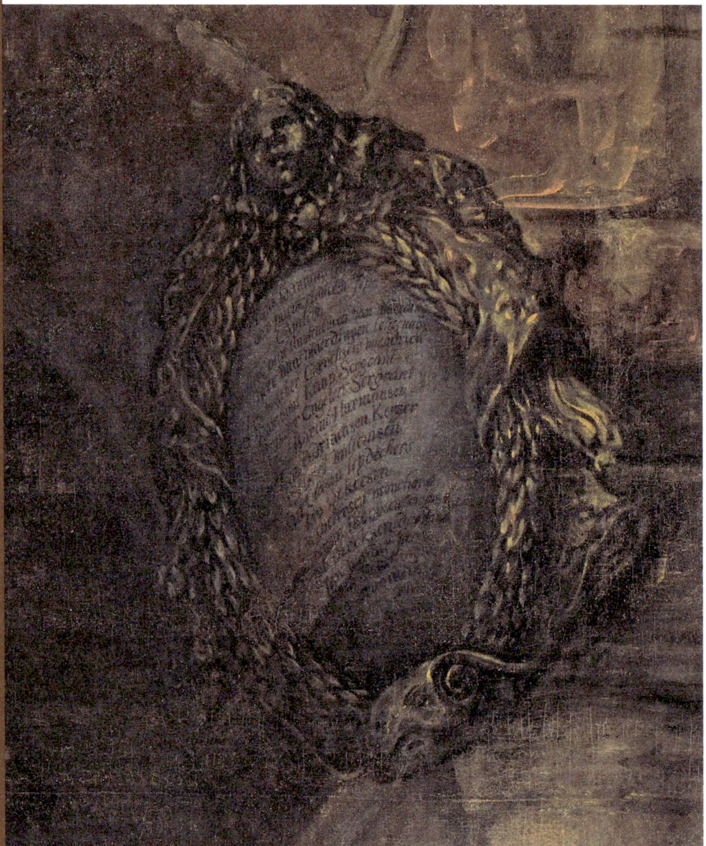

**15**
Detail from the *Night Watch* of the shield with the civic guardsmen's names

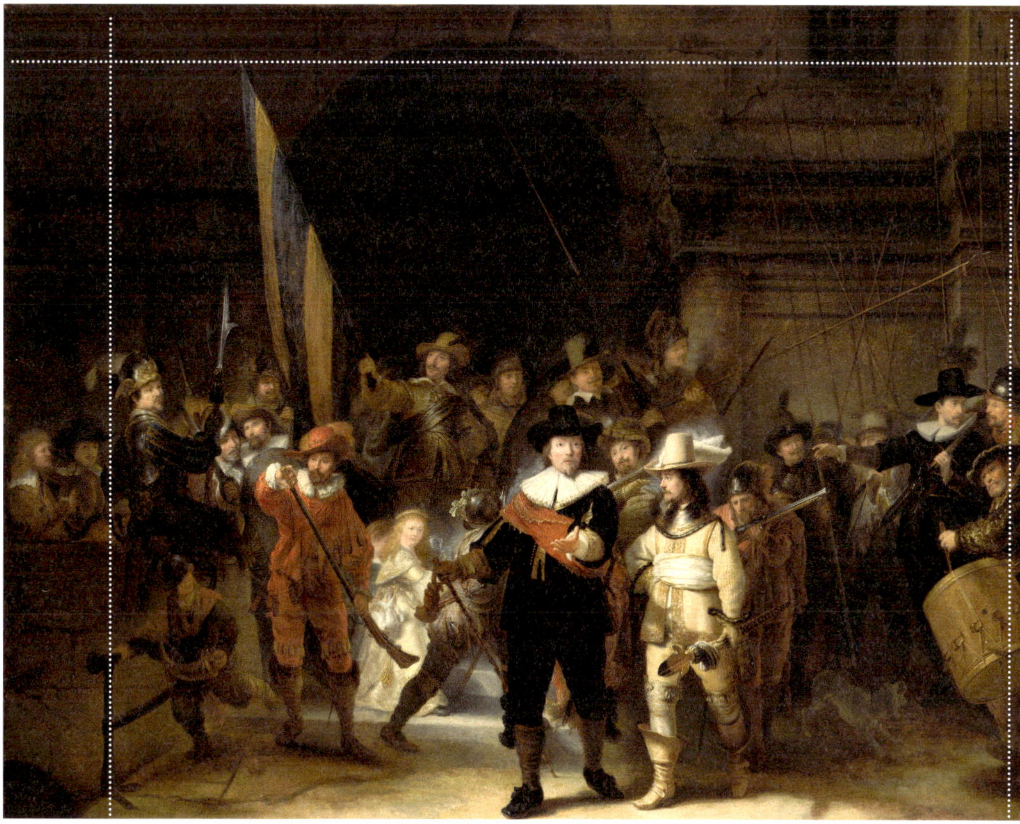

**16**
Attributed to Gerrit Lundens,
*The Night Watch*, c. 1642–1683.
Oil on panel, 66.5 × 85.5 cm.
Amsterdam, Rijksmuseum,
inv. no. SK-C-1453; on loan from
the National Gallery, London

The dotted lines indicate where
*The Night Watch* was cut down

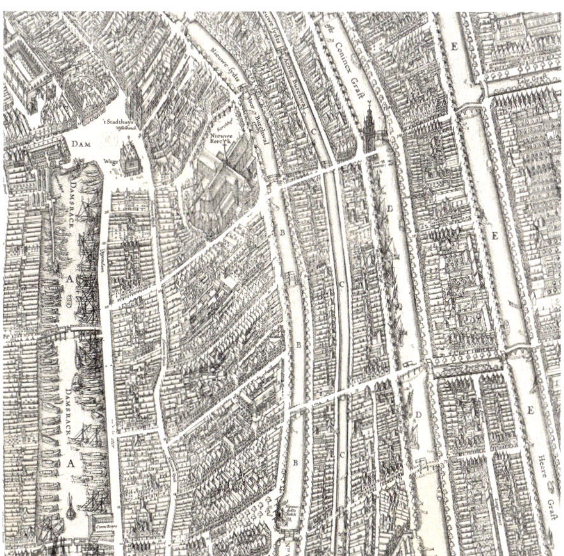


**17**
Balthazar Floris, *Map of
Amsterdam* (detail), 1625. Etching.
Amsterdam, Rijksmuseum,
inv. no. RP-P-1892-A-17491D

District II was situated to the north
of the Nieuwe Kerk (to the right
of Dam Square)

background and we only see the backs of their heads [FIG. 9]. The simplest way to identify the guardsmen and the extras in *The Night Watch* is to look at an etching of the painting on which the figures are numbered [FIG. 21].

The guardsmen Rembrandt portrayed belonged to the company for district II [FIG. 17], but only a small fraction of the entire troop, which may have had as many as 200 guardsmen, appear in the painting. The most important figure is the captain, Frans Banninck Cocq (no. 1), who shares centre stage with his lieutenant, Wilhem van Ruytenburch (no. 2). Banninck Cocq is elegantly dressed in black, with tassels under the knees of his breeches, a flat ruffled collar lavishly trimmed with lace, and a gold brocade shirt. This was the typical outfit of a married man from the regent class at the time. Upon closer inspection it becomes apparent that the captain is also wearing a metal collar, called a gorget, under his lace collar. This and the sword at his side denote his military role, as does the baton in his right hand, which identifies him as the captain. He also wears a red sash. Rembrandt may have deliberately chosen this colour so that, combined with the black of his costume and the white of his lace collar, Banninck Cocq symbolizes the city of Amsterdam, whose coat of arms is white, black and red [FIG. 18].

While Banninck Cocq wears the colours of the city of Amsterdam, Lieutenant Wilhem van Ruytenburch (no. 2) wears those of the Kloveniersdoelen, yellow and blue. Unlike Banninck Cocq's dress there is nothing civilian about Van Ruytenburch's clothing. Like the majority of guardsmen in the portraits by Pickenoy and Backer in the great hall, Van Ruytenburch wears a yellow leather coat, known as a buff coat, over a doublet with white-and-yellow striped sleeves. His breeches are also made of yellow leather and he has a highly ornamented gorget around his neck. Unlike the captain, who has on town shoes, he wears riding boots with spurs. The coat of arms of Amsterdam – three St Andrew's crosses, held by a lion – appears twice in the sumptuously embroidered border of his buff coat: a gorgeous touch [FIG. 19]. Van Ruytenburch carries the ceremonial weapon associated with the rank of lieutenant, a broad-bladed spear with pointed wings known as a partisan.

Next in rank was Jan Cornelisz Visscher (no. 3), the bearer of the company's standard. Such ensigns were required to come from wealthy families, and because their duty was to march into battle, lightly armed, and defend the standard at all costs, they had to be bachelors so there was no risk of them leaving behind a widow and children. Visscher, who was rich and never married, met these requirements with flying colours. The ensign usually cuts the most dashing figure in civic guard portraits, but with the exception of Van der Helst's splendid silver-clad standard bearer [FIG. 20], those in the paintings produced for the great hall are rather plain. Visscher looks up proudly at the company's banner, with the city's coat of arms held by a lion in the centre. The turquoise and yellow are repeated in his doublet and sash.

The troop's two sergeants have been placed almost symmetrically on either side of the painting. Although they had the same civic guard function, the way they are dressed makes them polar opposites. Rombout Kemp on the right (no. 5) wears a contemporary black costume similar to the one worn by Captain Banninck Cocq, with a millstone ruff and a broad-brimmed hat. The weapon he holds, a halberd, has a metal blade with an axe on one side and a hook on the other. The halberd was designed in the fourteenth century so that foot soldiers could pull cavalrymen off their mounts, but in the seventeenth century it was used by sergeants to keep their men in line. The model held by Kemp was of contemporary manufacture. In contrast to Kemp, Sergeant Reijer Jansz Engelen (no. 4), seated on a parapet on what is now the far left of the painting, comes across as an altogether archaic type. He wears a cuirass and has a gauntlet on his right hand. His very ornate helmet is based on Italian Renaissance models, but may well have sprouted from Rembrandt's imagination. The halberd Engelen holds is also at least a century old.

Since Ketel's 1588 painting, almost all civic guard portraits included the captain, lieutenant, ensign and two sergeants with the weapons associated with their rank. Rembrandt did not deviate from this pattern, although the way Engelen is outfitted is highly unusual. Some of the other guardsmen in Rembrandt's painting, however, carry arms that either never, or only very occasionally, appear in other militia pieces. In fact, there is a wider variety of weapons in *The Night Watch* than in any other civic guard portrait. A number of them were no longer in use and the costumes worn by the men who handle them also hark back to an earlier era in some instances. Another unusual feature of Rembrandt's work is that no fewer than nine guardsmen wear helmets, whereas there is not a single helmeted figure in the other paintings that hung in the great hall.

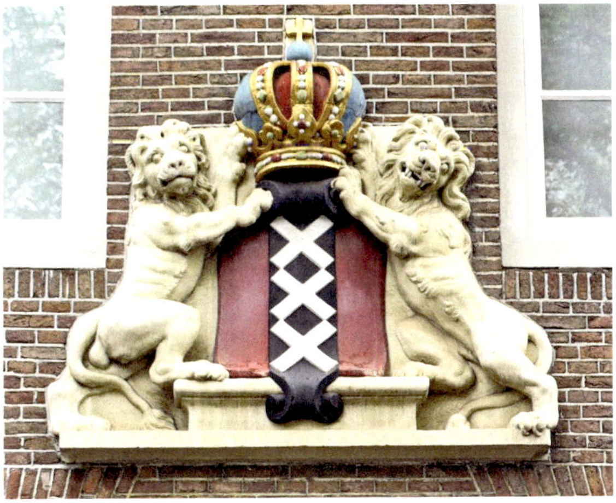

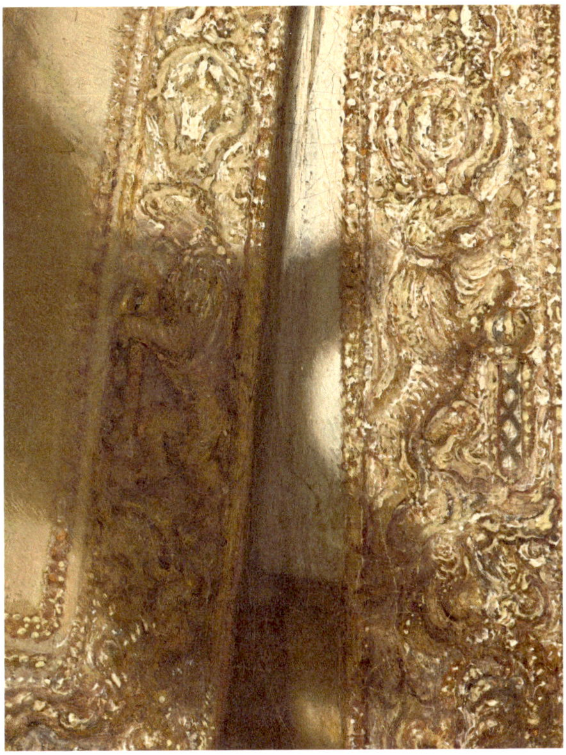

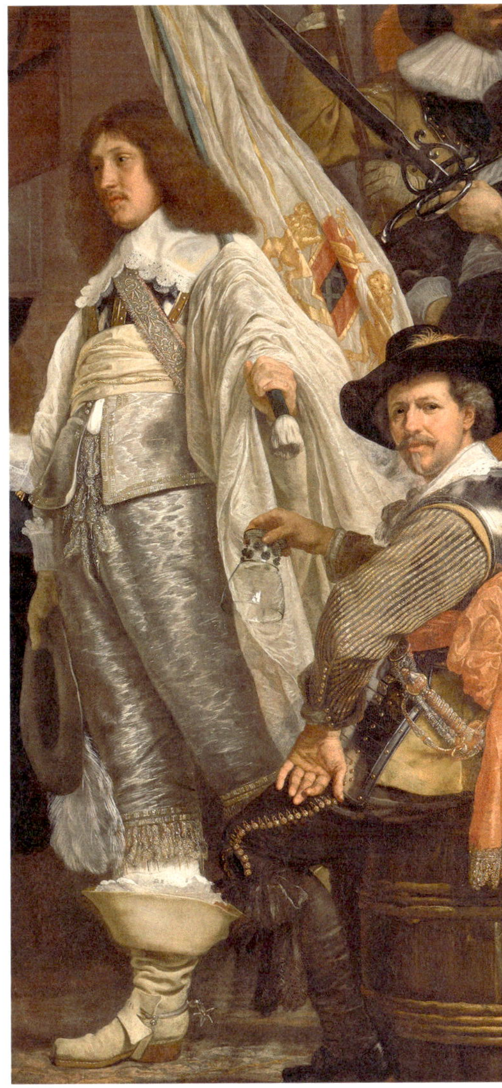

20
Detail of the company's ensign, Pieter Hulft, from Van der Helst's civic guard portrait [FIG. 10]

18
The Amsterdam coat of arms

19
Detail of the Amsterdam coat of arms on Lieutenant Wilhem van Ruytenburch's buff coat

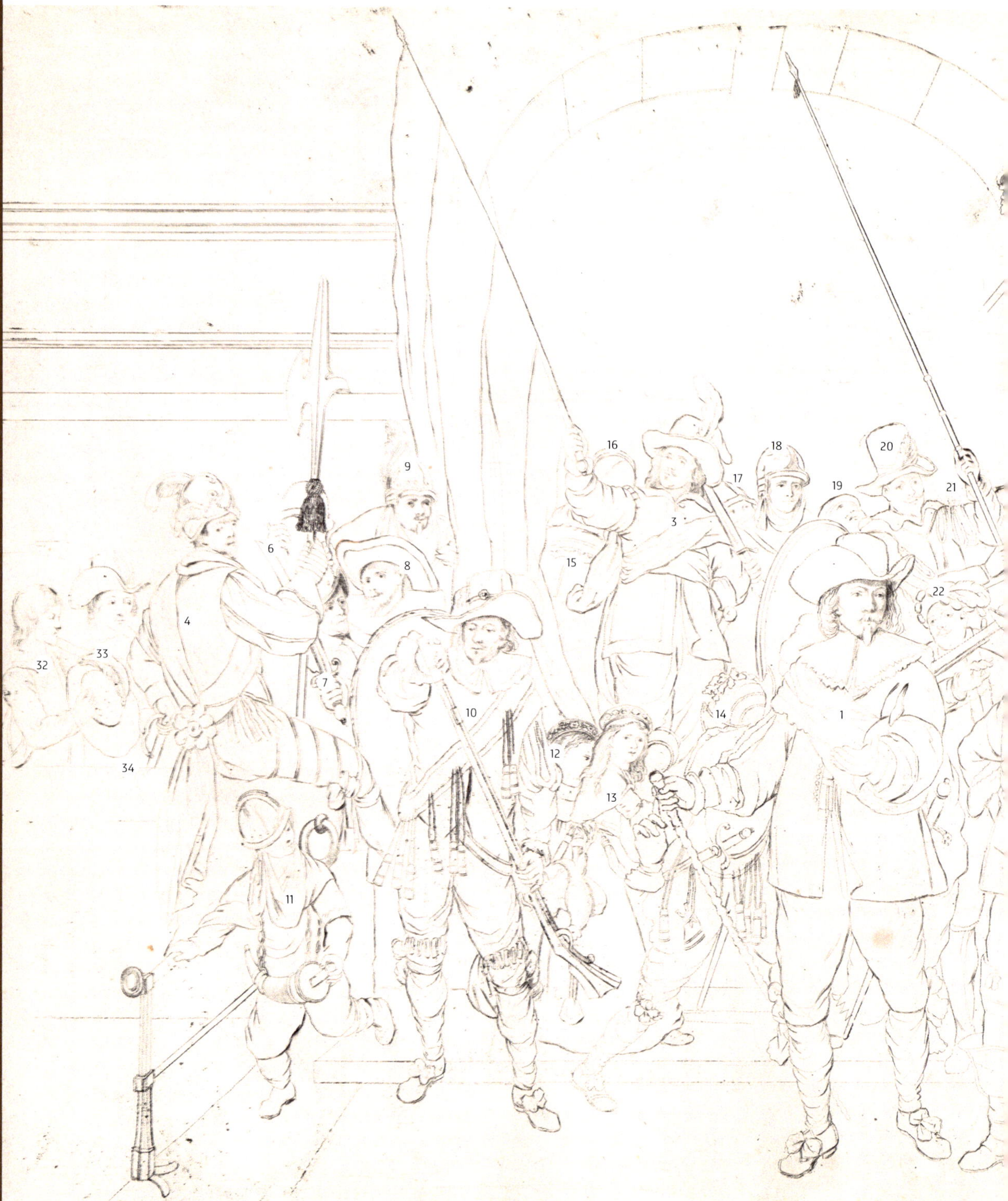
16
18
20
9
17
19
21
3
6
8
15
22
4
33
32
7
10
14
1
12
34
13
11

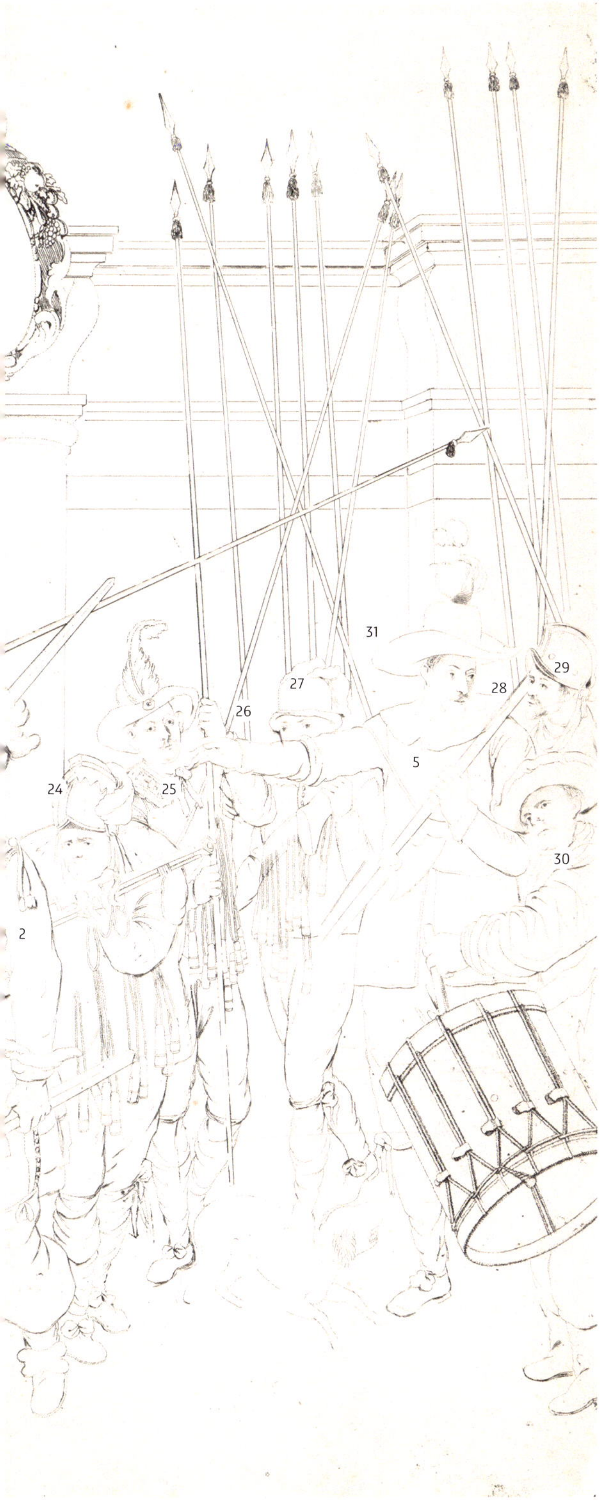


**21**
Lambertus Claessens,
*The Night Watch*, 1797. Etching
(first state), 467 x 625 mm.
Amsterdam, Rijksmuseum,
inv. no. RP-P-1883-A-7355

The numbers and the key are taken from Egbert Haverkamp Begemann's 1982 book on *The Night Watch*. The officers in *The Night Watch* can be identified on the basis of their weapons. The identities of some of the guardsmen have been established by comparison with other portraits of them. The rest have been tentatively identified by the former Amsterdam city archivist, S.A.C. Dudok van Heel

1. Captain Frans Banninck Cocq (1605–1655), Lord of Purmerland and Ilpendam
2. Lieutenant Wilhem van Ruytenburch (1600–1652), Lord of Vlaardingen
3. Ensign Jan Cornelisz Visscher (1610–1650)
4. Sergeant Reijer Jansz Engelen (1588–1651)
5. Sergeant Rombout Kemp (1597–1653)
6. Musketeer
7. Rondassier: possibly Jan Pietersz Bronckhorst (1587–after 1666)
8. Rondassier: Herman Jacobsz Wormskerck (1590–1653)
9. Musketeer with gun-fork and slow-match: possibly Elbert Willemsz Swedenrijck (1589–1644)
10. Musketeer loading his weapon: possibly Jan Aertsz van der Heede (1610–1655)
11. Powder boy
12. Girl in blue
13. Girl in gold
14. Musketeer firing his weapon
15. Head of a man
16. Head of a man
17. Head of a man
18. Rondassier: possibly Claes van Cruysbergen (1613–1663)
19. Head of a man
20. Guardsman holding cavalry lance: possibly Jan Ockersen (1599–1652)
21. Head of a man
22. Captain of arms: possibly Jan Adriaensz Keijser (1594–1664)
23. Pikeman: Walich Schellingwou (1613–1653)
24. Musketeer blowing the pan clean of unexploded powder: possibly Jan Claesen Leijdeckers (1597–1640)
25. Pikeman: possibly Barent Haermensz Bolhamer (1589–1661)
26. Head of a pikeman
27. Musketeer
28. Head of a man
29. Pikeman: possibly Paulus Harmensz Schoonhoven (1595–1679)
30. Drummer: probably Jacob Jorisz (1591–after 1646)
31. Head of a man
32. Musketeer (in section removed c. 1715): possibly Jan Brughman (1614–1652)
33. Man with a hat (in section removed c. 1715): possibly Jan Dircksz de Roy (1601–1659)
34. Child peering over a parapet (in section removed c. 1715)

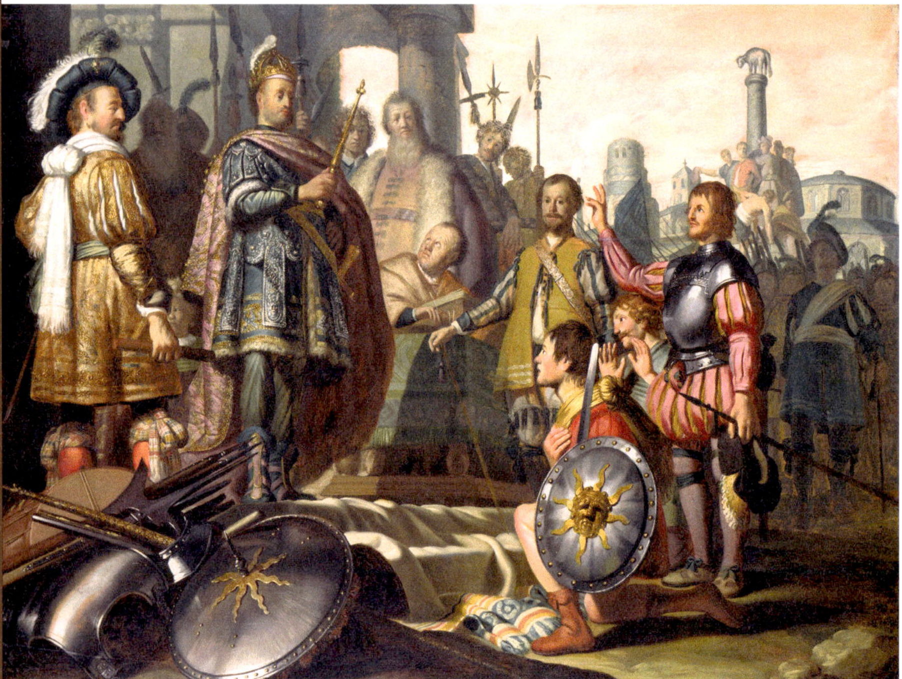

**22**
Rembrandt van Rijn, *History Painting*, 1626. Oil on panel, 89.8 × 121 cm. Leiden, Stedelijk Museum De Lakenhal, inv. no. B 564

**23**
Detail of the captain of arms holding a two-handed sword, from Van der Helst's civic guard portrait [FIG 10]

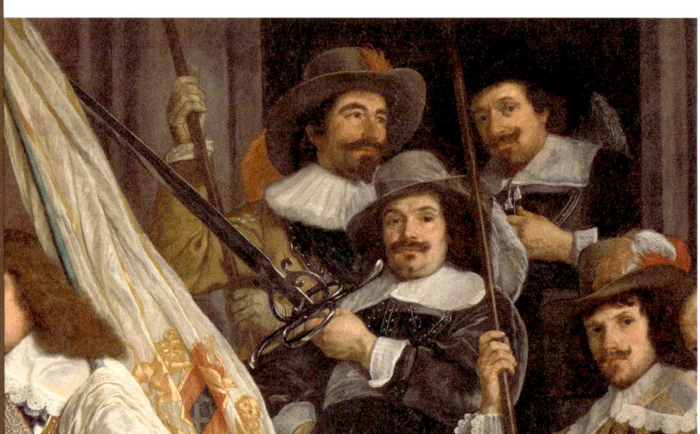

The guardsman to the right of Ensign Visscher carries a sword and round shield, known as a *rondas*, from which this type of soldier derived the name *rondassier* (no. 18). *The Night Watch* is the only militia portrait since 1596 to include such a figure, and, as if to underline the fact, this one wears a late sixteenth-century helmet. Another *rondassier* stands to the left of the company's banner, wearing contemporary clothing (no. 8). The soft hat with notched brim worn by the guardsman between Captain Banninck Cocq and Lieutenant van Ruytenburch (no. 22) is also a sixteenth-century costume item. From the very beginning of his career, Rembrandt used this kind of apparel from the previous century in his paintings of Old Testament and mythological subjects, as well as subjects derived from Ancient Roman history [FIG. 22]. His use of it here is one of the reasons why *The Night Watch* looks more like a history painting than a portrait. The two-handed sword held by the figure with the old-fashioned hat identifies him as a captain of arms, a non-commissioned officer responsible for the care of weapons. Rembrandt was the first artist in almost fifty years to include this unwieldy sword in a militia portrait. Van der Helst may have followed Rembrandt's lead in this respect in his 1643 painting in the great hall [FIG. 23].

The fellow wearing a top hat just behind Rembrandt's captain of arms holds what appears to be a very long cavalry lance (no. 20). No other civic guard portrait includes one. This is not the case with the pike, one of the weapons that figure most prominently in *The Night Watch*. There are fifteen of them – but only two pikemen – on the right side of the painting. Pikes were still very much in use in Rembrandt's day and, just as he depicted them, pikemen were concentrated in groups when engaged in battle as well as when on parade [FIG. 11]. Pikes in this number do not often appear in civic guard pieces, but Rembrandt was not the only artist to use them in this way. Van der Helst and especially Backer [FIGS. 10, 9] also realized, perhaps even better than Rembrandt, that a few pikes in the background of one's painting go a long way in creating the illusion that a much larger group of men is present than is actually the case.

By far the most important type of arms in *The Night Watch* is the musket. The most effective weapon in warfare since the end of the sixteenth century, it was eventually used by all civic guard companies irrespective of which *doelen* they were associated with. However, the musket had been the assigned weapon of the Kloveniers ever since the foundation of the guild in 1522, and for this reason it features prominently in *The Night Watch* and in four of the six other civic guard portraits that were made for the great hall. In Rembrandt's painting, seven figures hold muskets, while on the right we can make out the parallel barrels of three more muskets whose bearers are blocked from view by Sergeant Kemp. Three musketeers (nos. 10, 14, 24) form a conspicuous row directly behind Captain Banninck Cocq and Lieutenant van Ruytenburch. Together, they illustrate three consecutive stages in the handling of the musket derived from a very influential book by Jacques de Gheyn first published in 1607, and later translated into English under the title *The Exercise of Armes*. The two musketeers dressed in red are guardsmen, although the costume worn by the one on the left (no. 10) has a rather sixteenth-century look about it. Seen in full, this figure is loading his musket with gunpowder from one of the wooden cartridges attached to his bandolier [FIG. 24]. The guardsman in red behind Lieutenant van Ruytenburch (no. 24) is clearing the pan of his musket by blowing off the excess powder that remained there after the weapon was fired [FIGS. 25, 26].

## A BOY IN PURPLE PADDED HOSE AND A GIRL WITH A CHICKEN

The oddest looking of the three musketeers in the row behind Captain Banninck Cocq and Lieutenant van Ruytenburch is the boy in the middle (no. 14), who fires the only shot in the picture. Between the captain and the lieutenant we can make out the barrel of his musket, the plume of smoke that issues from it melding with the feathers in Van Ruytenburch's hat. The illustration in De Gheyn's book that served as the model for this pose was also used by Van der Helst for his painting in the great hall [FIGS. 27, 28]. His musketeer differs from Rembrandt's in that he has not yet let off his weapon. Muskets are, however, being fired in the background of both Van der Helst's and Backer's works, and by one of the guardsmen in Pickenoy's portrait. There were thus four paintings in the great hall of the Kloveniersdoelen in which the musket was shown in action, which was another first, as the weapon is not discharged in any of the other civic guard paintings that have come down to us.

There are other, more important differences between the centrally placed musketeers in *The Night Watch* and Van der Helst's painting. In the latter

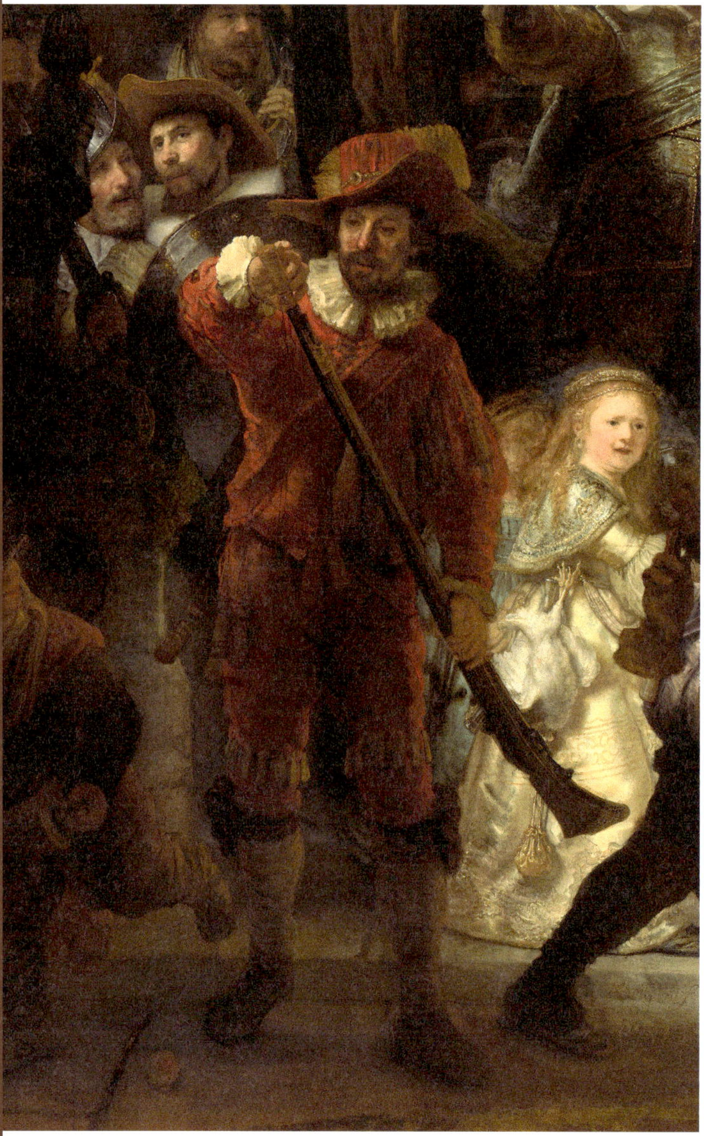

**24**
Detail of the musketeer loading
his weapon (no. 10)

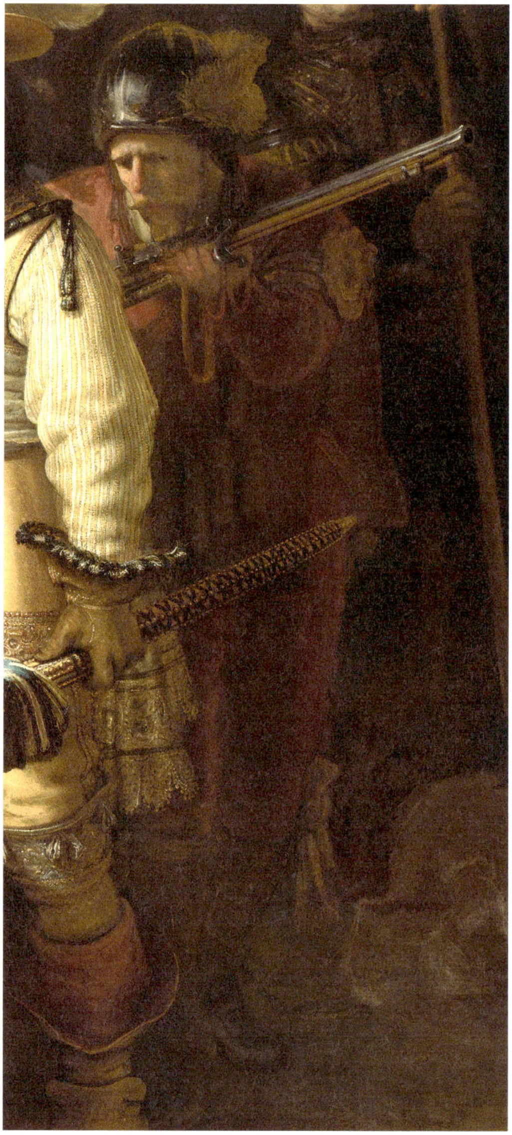

**25**
Detail of the guardsman,
to the right of Lieutenant
Wilhem van Ruytenburch (no. 24)
clearing the pan of his musket

**26**
Robert de Baudous after Jacques de Gheyn, *A Musketeer Blowing the Pan of his Weapon Clean of Unexploded Powder*, c. 1597–1607, from *The Excercise of Armes*. Engraving, 260 × 181 mm. Amsterdam, Rijksmuseum, inv. no. RP-P-OB-52.641

**27**
Robert de Baudous after Jacques de Gheyn, *A Musketeer Firing his Weapon*, c. 1597–1607, from *The Exercise of Armes*. Engraving, 263 × 193 mm. Amsterdam, Rijksmuseum, inv. no. RP-P-OB-52.713

Compare the boy in the purple padded hose (no. 14)

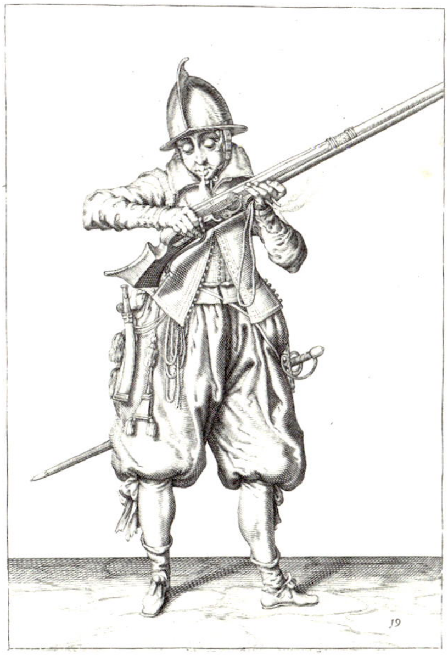


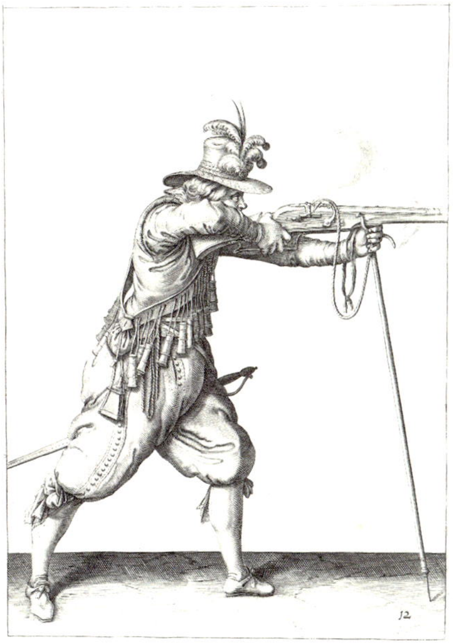


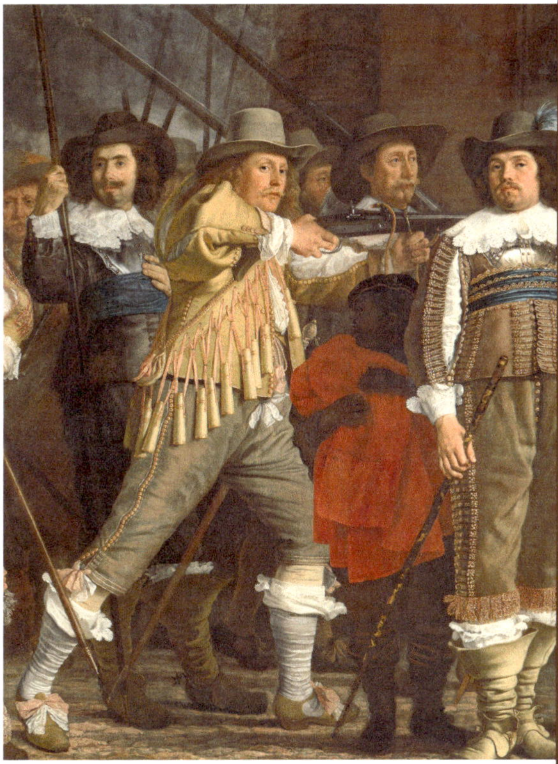

**28**
Detail of the guardsman about to fire his musket, from Van der Helst's civic guard portrait [FIG. 10]

work the musketeer wears the fashions of his time, including a buff coat, while the purple padded hose and helmet worn by Rembrandt's musketeer are from the 1590s. Whereas Van der Helst's musketeer looks at us, the face of Rembrandt's is hidden from sight. Van der Helst's musketeer has the individual features of one of the civic guardsmen he was commissioned to portray, but Rembrandt's does not have a face and is therefore not an individual but the representation of an entire group. He is a symbolic figure, a personification of musketry, and the oak leaves adorning his helmet are a symbol of the strength of the musketeers and the civic guardsmen in general, as well as the victory that the firearm will bring them [FIG. 29].

The faceless musketeer is only one of sixteen extras in *The Night Watch*, most of whom are just fragments of figures – an eye and part of a nose – filling the gaps between the guardsmen who paid to have their portraits included in the painting. The fragmentary head to the right of Ensign Visscher probably belongs to Rembrandt (no. 17), who spent years standing in front of the painting while he worked on it, but now appears at the rear of the crowd regarding us, the viewers, as we look at him at the back of the painting in a never-ending exchange of glances. The partially glimpsed supernumeraries go a long way towards suggesting the presence of the entire troop. Among the few extras to be given a more important role is the drummer on the right (no. 30). He was not a member of the company, but was hired for special occasions such as parades. His soft hat and slashed sleeves give him a sixteenth-century air.

As intriguing as the boy in the purple hose, if not more so, are the two girls to the left of him (nos. 12, 13). As a centre of light, the one dressed in gold irresistibly draws our attention, and her slightly blurry appearance and magnificent dress make her seem a mysterious apparition [FIG. 29]. She wears an imaginary costume composed of a long, finely brocaded robe with a separate cape, but the most unusual thing about her is the large white fowl, most likely a chicken, hanging upside down by its claws from her dress. The girl also has a pistol. Rembrandt probably got the idea for this figure from prints and paintings depicting sutlers, women who accompanied troops on the move, peddling provisions to the soldiers [FIG. 30]. It is tempting to consider the child wearing the oversized helmet in one of these prints as the source for the cutest extra in Rembrandt's painting, the little boy on the left dashing off with a powder horn (no. 11).

Like the boy in the purple hose, the girl in gold is a symbolic figure. The firearm hanging from her belt was the privileged weapon of the Kloveniers and the claws of the fowl at her waist also refer to their headquarters. As the emblem of the Kloveniersdoelen, the golden claw could be seen everywhere in and on the building itself. Flinck too included it in his portrait of the *doelen*'s governors painted in the same year as *The Night Watch* [FIG. 31]. While the boy in the purple padded hose personifies musketry, the girl with the chicken symbolizes the Kloveniers themselves.

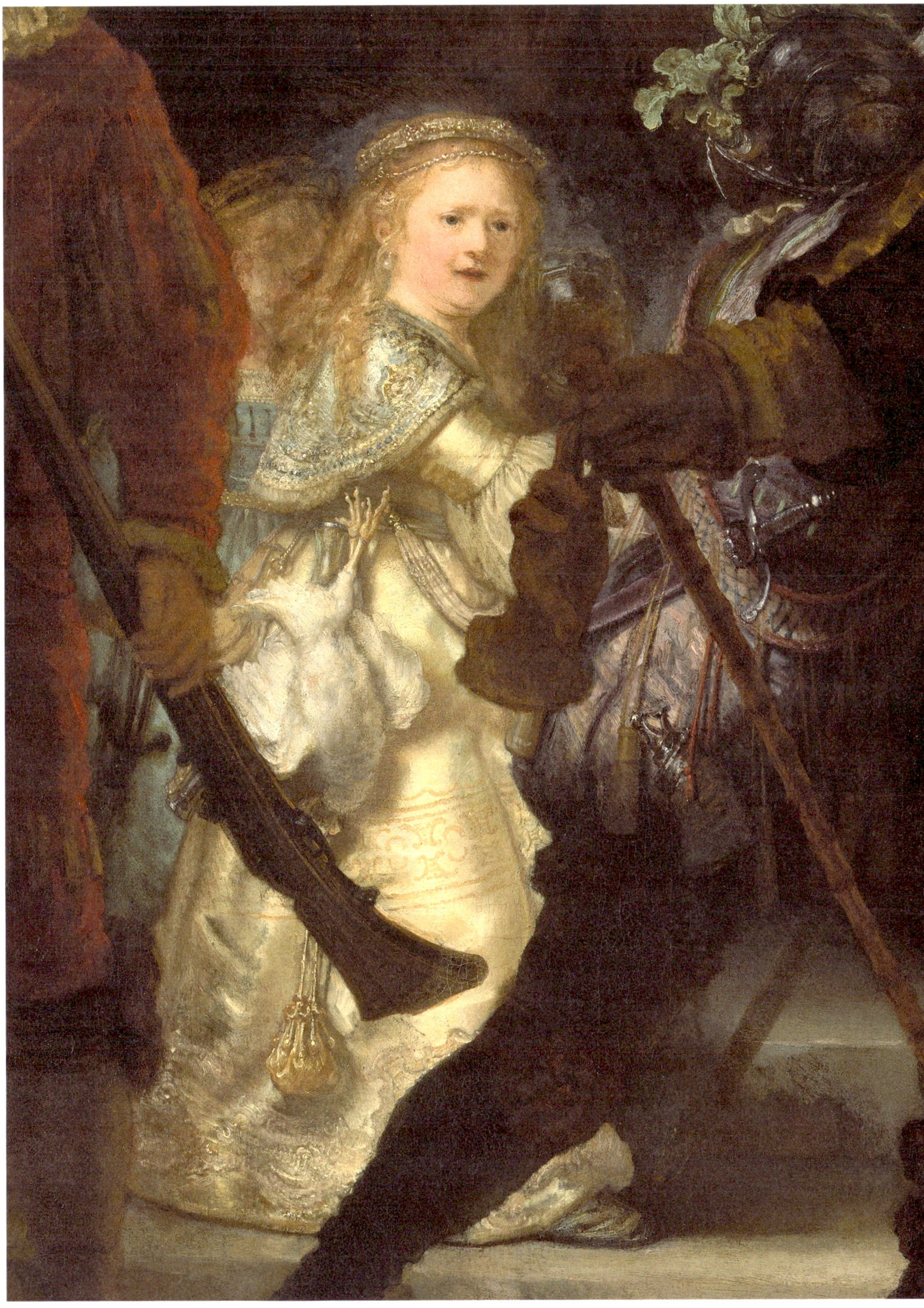

**29**
Detail of the girl, with the chicken at her waist (no. 13) and the musketeer in the purple hose (no. 14)

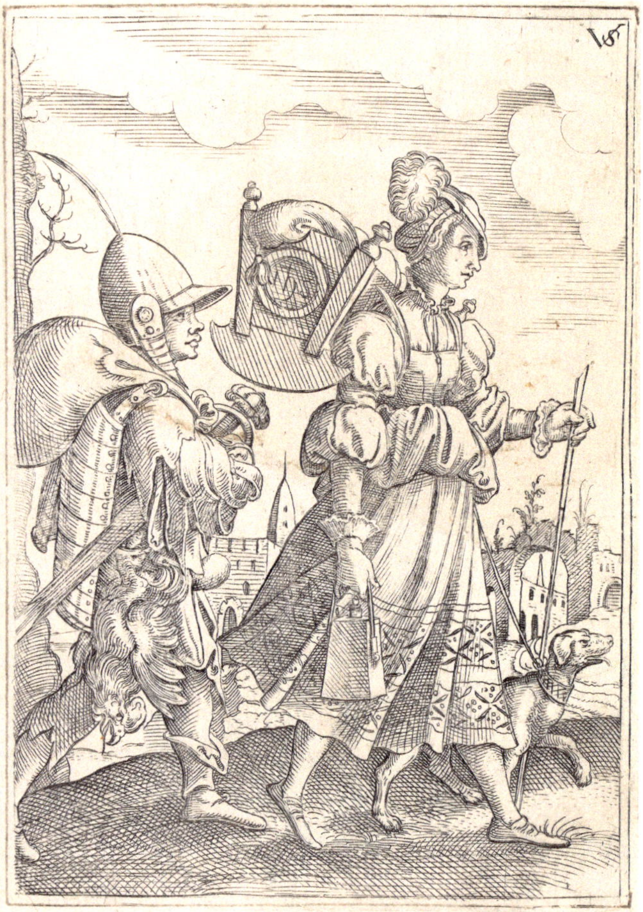

**30**
Virgil Solis, *A Sutler and her Assistant*, c. 1530–1555. Engraving, 112 × 80 mm. London, British Museum, inv. no. 1850,0612.478

While the sutler herself does not carry the chicken in this print, the puffed sleeves and decorative bands of her dress are costume elements she shares with Rembrandt's girl (no. 13)

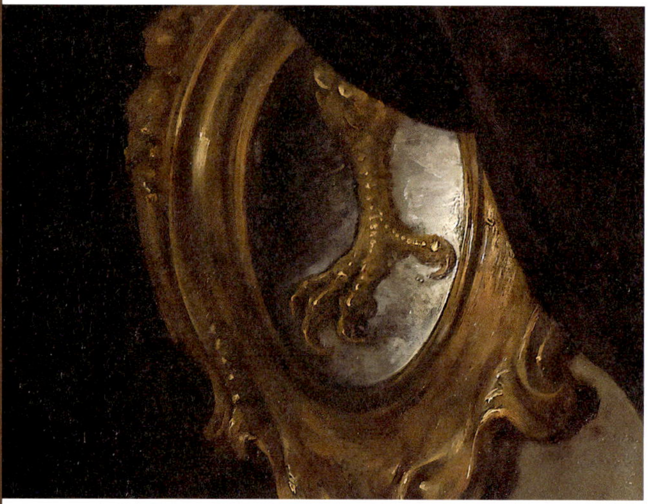

**31**
Detail of the emblem of the Kloveniersdoelen from Flinck's governors portrait [FIG. 5]

## ACTION!

One of the things about *The Night Watch* that Baldinucci (or his informant Keil) admired was the way the captain appears to be moving. A calligraphic inscription on the page opposite a drawing after the painting in Banninck Cocq's own family album [FIG. 32] also mentions this action. 'The young Lord of Purmerland, as captain, orders his lieutenant, the Lord of Vlaardingen, to march out his company of civic guardsmen'. With his bare left hand he gives the command, and the guardsmen scramble to get into line. Action is implied not only by the actual animation of the figures, such as the little boy on the left running to keep up with the guardsmen, but also by way of gestures, the direction of glances, and the movement of clothing and objects. Sergeant Kemp (no. 5), for example, points the way the guardsmen must go and Captain Banninck Cocq's sash swings behind him, as do the cartridges suspended from the bandolier of the musketeer who is loading his weapon (no. 10). And all this activity is accompanied by noise. We can almost hear the drumming, the musket being fired and the dog barking.

*The Night Watch* is the only civic guard portrait in which action is the governing principle. In this respect, a greater contrast between Rembrandt's and Pickenoy's paintings can hardly be imagined. Although a few of the guardsmen in the latter work load or shoot their muskets, there is none of the dynamism that we find in *The Night Watch*. Not only are the guardsmen neatly lined up in a row, but also their heads are all on the same level. In *The Night Watch*, on the other hand, the figures have been placed on various levels, making much more use of the available picture surface. Nor do Rembrandt's figures occupy only the foreground of the painting, as they do in Pickenoy's. In order to achieve this more ambitious arrangement of the guardsmen and the extras in space, Rembrandt created an architectural setting that is not entirely logical. What, for example, are the men in the centre background, among them Ensign Visscher and the guardsman wearing a tall hat, standing on? Supposedly there is a flight of stairs here, the lowest being visible between the legs of the boy in the purple hose, but these figures are far too elevated for the steps to make real sense.

The action in the painting and the arrangement of the figures on different levels are two other aspects that make *The Night Watch* resemble a history piece more than a group portrait. The latter was also a strategy recommended in the most well-known instruction manual for young Dutch artists at the time, Karel van Mander's *Schilder-Boeck* (Book on Painting), which had been published in 1604. The author suggested this in the chapter of his book entitled 'On the composition and invention of history pieces' ('Over de ordening en de inventie van de historiestukken'), likening it to how market stallholders display their wares. Rembrandt heeded yet another piece of Van Mander's advice to history painters. In order to add richness and variety in a scene, the artist was to include animals and people of different ages, such as 'fresh youths and beautiful young maidens, old men, matrons, and children of all ages'. This was the reason why Rembrandt did not limit himself to depicting only the eighteen civic guardsmen of district II.

But by using so many figures, and by distributing them on various levels and positions in space, the artist created a significant challenge for himself: how to maintain unity in what is a scene of seeming chaos. Critics later noted that Rembrandt achieved this admirably well. He accomplished it chiefly by placing inlets of space on either side of Banninck Cocq and Van Ruytenburch. The figures behind the captain and lieutenant have been set on two main diagonals, which are reinforced by a series of smaller ones. The company's standard, the musket held by the guardsman in red and the baton held by Banninck Cocq himself, for example, are all set on diagonals pointing towards the captain. On the right side, similar diagonals are formed by Van Ruytenburch's partisan, the musket held by the figure behind him and other weapons. Sergeant Kemp's right arm and even the drum have been positioned so that they create diagonals. Everything leads the eye to Captain Banninck Cocq, and as if this was not enough to tell us that he is the most important figure in the painting, he is shown significantly larger than his lieutenant. But these diagonals do more than emphasize the captain's status; they also help propel the action forward in the direction the company will march.

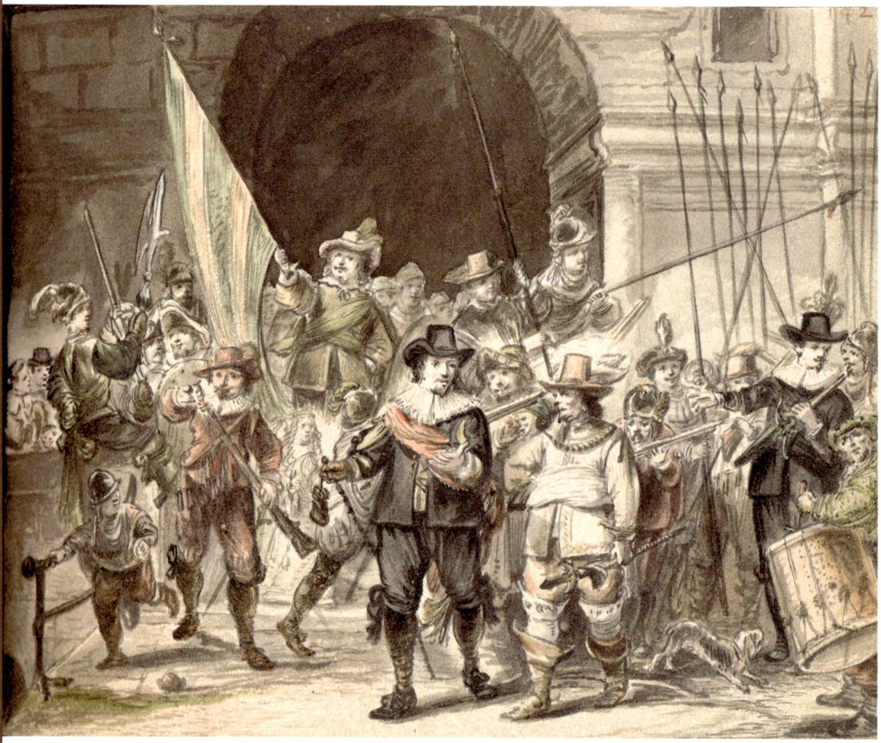

**32**
Attributed to Jacob Colijns, *Drawing of the Night Watch in the Banninck Cocq Family Album*. Amsterdam, Rijksmuseum, inv. no. SK-C-1102

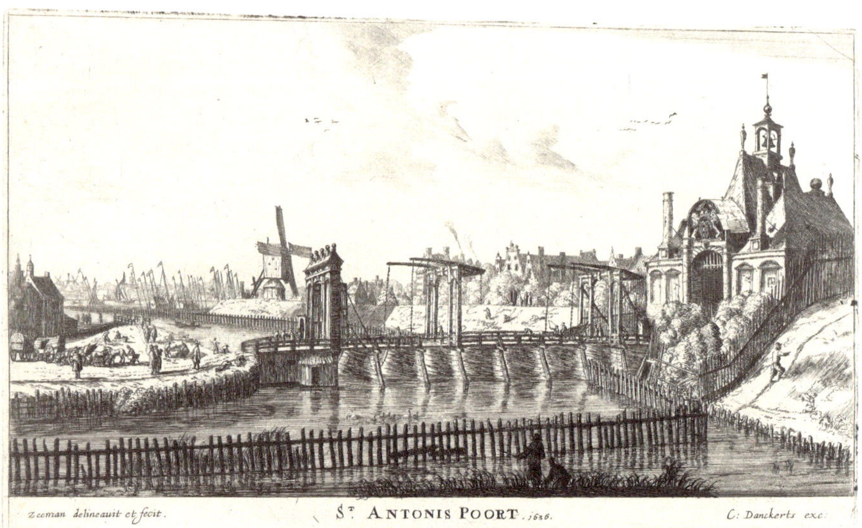


**33**
Reinier Nooms, *Sint-Antoniespoort*, c. 1652–1656. Etching and drypoint, 180 × 302 mm. Amsterdam, Rijksmuseum, inv. no. RP-P-OB-20.583

## LIGHT AND SHADOW, AND HOW THE NIGHT WATCH GOT ITS NAME

Whereas the light in all other civic guard portraits is evenly distributed, much of *The Night Watch* is cast in shadow with spotlights shining on the main figures. Most of the light is concentrated on Banninck Cocq, whose open right hand seems to catch it, and Van Ruytenburch, who is the brightest figure in the composition. The girl with the chicken is also highly illuminated, but it is not clear what the source of this light is. Like a true apparition, she appears to be generating it herself. The irregular pattern of light and shade in the painting creates a sense of drama and adds to the overall dynamism of the scene. It is no wonder that, in the early nineteenth century, the Dutch painter Quirinus van Amelsfoort regarded this 'mysterious' light as more suitable to a religious work than a portrait of civic guardsmen.

A relatively dark painting to begin with, the accumulation of dirt and layers of varnish made *The Night Watch* even darker as time went by. Past treatments of the work only made matters worse. According to the painter, restorer and supervisor of the art collection of the city of Amsterdam, Jan van Dijk, in 1758, 'because of the great deal of boiled Oil and Varnishes that have from time to time been brushed over it ... one thought it was covered with tar'. The condition of *The Night Watch* was likely one of the factors that led to the misconception that the soldiers in the portrait are patrolling at night – although Van Dijk himself carried out a major restoration in 1751–1752, which presumably improved the picture's appearance. The first recorded use of the title *The Night Watch* dates to 1797, but it may have already been called that for some time. It was probably not only the work's condition that led to this name, but also the fact that in the eighteenth century virtually the only task left to the civic guard was just that – night patrols.

## THE SETTING AND THE PAINTING'S MEANING

Captain Banninck Cocq has given Lieutenant van Ruytenburch the order to march the company out. But why? Perhaps the archway from which the troop emerges can provide an answer. Advocates of the theory that *The Night Watch* is related to Maria de' Medici's visit to Amsterdam have likened this architectural backdrop to the triumphal arches that were erected in her honour [FIG. 11], but the resemblance is only superficial. A better comparison can be made with Sint-Antoniespoort [FIG. 33], one of the gates to the city where the civic guard stood watch. But here, too, we do not have a perfect match. Nevertheless, in the context of Rembrandt's painting it makes more sense that the structure is a city gate rather than one of the temporary arches erected in 1638. Maria de' Medici's visit was not the only time Amsterdam's militia companies could be seen on parade. Once a year, on Sundays in the summer, the civic guard companies would take turns marching to Dam Square where they would fire their muskets. *The Night Watch* is not simply an illustration of one of these military tattoos, for the inclusion of purely symbolic figures in the painting, representing the Kloveniersdoelen and the art of musketry, raises it far above such mundane events. Nor are the archaic costumes worn by the extras and some of the guardsmen parade outfits, as has often been claimed; on the contrary, they are a reminder of the long and venerable history of Amsterdam's militia. Nevertheless, the marching in the painting does serve the same purpose as the annual parades, which was to demonstrate the civic guard's readiness and ability to defend the city against attack. Viewed in this light, the gate in the background of *The Night Watch* also has a symbolic function: it stands for the city of Amsterdam. The key to understanding *The Night Watch* is hidden in the shadow cast by the captain's outstretched left hand that cups the coat of arms of Amsterdam embroidered on the border of Van Ruytenburch's coat [FIG. 19]. This, of course, is exactly what Banninck Cocq and his men were doing by defending Amsterdam from its enemies: they were holding the city in their protective hands. This is why the men stand in front of an imaginary city gate as they hurry to get into formation and march out to fight for their beloved city.

## WHO WERE THE EIGHTEEN CIVIC GUARDSMEN?

Except for the captain and lieutenant, all of the eighteen guardsmen portrayed by Rembrandt lived in district II itself. The majority were members of the Reformed Church, while one of the portrayed guardsmen, Jan Aertsz van der Heede (no. 10), belonged to the more liberal Remonstrant Confession, and two were Catholics, Barent Harmansz Bolhamer and Jan Dircksz de Roy (nos. 25 and 33). The latter even served as governor of the Roman Catholic Aged Poor Relief Office from 1628 to 1654.

Some civic guard districts were known for a certain industry that was concentrated there. The herring trade, for example, was located in district V, whose civic guardsmen are represented in the portrait Jacob Backer painted for the great hall of the Kloveniersdoelen. Six of his sitters were involved in this business, including one of the sergeants, who had the very fitting last name Visch (the Dutch word for fish). One of the sitters in *The Night Watch*, Elbert Willem Swedenrijck (no. 9), was also a fishmonger, but the majority of the guardsmen in Rembrandt's painting – eight of them in all – were cloth merchants, including Jan Brughman (no. 32), who was the scion of the richest family of district II. Some of them were new to the profession, such as Jan Pietersz Bronckhorst (no. 7), who worked himself up from cloth shearer to cloth merchant. Others practised different professions, but had relatives in the business. Wine merchant Wallich Schellingwou (no. 23), for instance, came from a family that had been in the cloth trade for some 80 years. A number of Rembrandt's guardsmen held important functions in the cloth guild. Herman Jacobsz Wormskerck (no. 8), for example, was its dean in 1628. Jan Dircksz de Roy (no. 33), Jan Ockersen (no. 20) and sergeant Rombout Kemp (no. 5) served seven or eight times as syndics, that is, sampling officials who judged the quality of the blue and black dyed cloths manufactured and sold by the guild members.

Neither Captain Frans Banninck Cocq nor Lieutenant Wilhem van Ruytenburch were involved in the cloth industry. Rather, both were lawyers, a profession often chosen by those with political ambitions. Banninck Cocq graduated with a degree in law from the university in Poitiers. From 1632, he held posts in the Amsterdam city government every year, eventually being appointed one of the city's four burgomasters for the first time in 1650. He owed his political career not only to his law degree, but especially to his family's multiple ties to the Hooft family, one of the most powerful in Amsterdam. With his 1630 wedding to Maria Overlander, whose mother was a member of the Hooft family, this bond became even stronger. Maria Overlander's sister Geertruid was, moreover, the first wife of Cornelis de Graeff (the captain in Backer's portrait), who together with his brother Andries dominated Amsterdam politics in the middle of the seventeenth century.

Wilhem van Ruytenburch's political career was far less spectacular than that of Banninck Cocq, primarily because he lacked the latter's connections to Amsterdam's ruling families. He was a member of the city council from 1639, and served as alderman in 1641 and commissioner for matrimonial affairs for three years (1642, 1643 and 1646). He owed his appointment in 1639 as lieutenant of district II to the fact that his sister was married to the brother of Pieter Reael, who was captain at the time. Van Ruytenburch would go on to become captain of district II himself in 1646, but in the following year he moved permanently to The Hague and Vlaardingen.

Banninck Cocq's military career was also more impressive than his lieutenant's. In 1635, the former had been appointed lieutenant of district I and rose to become captain of district II probably in early 1639. Around 1646, he was selected to be one of the two colonels in charge of the city's twenty civic guard companies, in which capacity he issued a new ordinance for the militia in 1650, among other things. In 1648, he became one of the governors of the Handboogdoelen (the headquarters of the longbowmen). A few of the other guardsmen made more minor advances in this hierarchy. Sergeant Rombout Kemp (no. 5) would go on to become lieutenant of district II in 1646. His son, Artus, succeeded Jan Cornelisz Visscher (no. 3), who died still unmarried in 1650, as standard bearer. In that year, the number of civic guard districts was increased from 20 to 54 and their borders redrawn. The streets on which Jan van der Heede (no. 10) and Jan Ockersen (no. 20) lived became part of the new district XXI, and they were appointed its new sergeant and lieutenant.

The captain and lieutenant were the only sitters to inherit titles: Van Ruytenburch became Lord of Vlaardingen when his father died in 1627, and Banninck Cocq became Lord of Purmerland and Ilpendam on the death of his father three years later.

## HOW THE PAINTING WAS JUDGED OVER THE YEARS

Given *The Night Watch*'s current status, it is amazing to learn that seventeenth-century guidebooks on Amsterdam describe the building and the room where the painting hung, but say nothing about the work itself. According to Filippo Baldinucci, however, it was with this picture that Rembrandt had 'acquired a greater name than almost any other artist from that region ever did'. As we have seen, Samuel van Hoogstraten was even convinced that it would 'outlive all of its rivals'. What struck Baldinucci, or at any rate his informant Bernard Keil, as extraordinary was the fact that there is movement in the painting and that the figures so convincingly recede into space. Van Hoogstraten praised the composition for 'being so pictorial in thought, so sinuous of step, and so forceful'. 'Sinuous of step' is one of a number of translations for the author's original Dutch phrase 'zwierich van sprong', which has no literal equivalent in any modern language. The expression has been convincingly interpreted as a reference to the snake-like movement of the figure groups on either side of Captain Frans Banninck Cocq and Lieutenant Wilhem van Ruytenburch. In his treatise, Van Hoogstraten insisted no fewer than three times that a composition should have this quality. The first time he wrote: 'It is not sufficient that a painter lines his figures up in rows next to each other, as one can see too often here in Holland in the meeting halls of the civic militias'. The second time he advised: 'Give your figures a pleasant arrangement [*sprong*], that is, an artful but seemingly non-artificial placement, so that one cannot, so to speak, behead them all with a single blow (as in some civic militia portraits)'. The former Rembrandt pupil was so obsessed with this issue, he felt it necessary to repeat it yet again: 'One shall provide the figures with a pleasing disposition [*sprong*] – that is, that they, be they tall or short, together form a shape that is pleasing to the eye, and that through their variety they seem to interact with one other and do not form disgusting rows.' As we have seen, Pickenoy's painting that hung next to *The Night Watch* was a prime example of these 'disgusting rows' of figures that can be 'beheaded with a single blow'.

Van Hoogstraten, however, was not enamoured of all of *The Night Watch*'s qualities. Rembrandt's light and dark contrasts were not to his taste and he would have preferred that his teacher 'had sparked a bit more light in it'. On the previous page of his book of rules, he confessed his predilection for the evenly lit pictures of Raphael and Michelangelo. In his opinion, 'the forced use of light and shadows is a feeble support' and it was 'an injustice to dim the one in order to enhance the other'.

In the eighteenth century, the tide turned in the appreciation of *The Night Watch*. With specific reference to Rembrandt's civic guard piece, the Dutch art collector Cornelis Ploos van Amstel wrote in 1767 that there was nothing exalted about his compositions, that his figures in general are of a low character and have a commoner's stature, and their draperies seldomly or never coincide with the period in which the scene takes place, but are rather the products of the artist's bizarre fantasy. Nor are his buildings lofty in appearance, but instead Gothic in style.

It was also in the eighteenth century that comparisons were first made between *The Night Watch* and Bartholomeus van der Helst's *Banquet of the Officers and Other Civic Guardsmen of District XVII in Amsterdam, under the Command of Captain Cornelis Jansz Witsen and Lieutenant Joan Oetgens van Waveren, in Celebration of the Peace of Münster, 10 June 1648* [FIG. 34]. The renowned English portraitist of the day, Sir Joshua Reynolds, lavished praise upon the latter in his *A Journey to Flanders and Holland in the Year 1781*, published in 1798: 'This is perhaps, the first picture, of portraits, in the world, comprehending more of those qualities which make a perfect portrait, than any other I have ever seen'. The Van der Helst 'far exceeded my expectation, as that of Rembrandt fell below it'. Reynolds even had difficulty persuading himself that *The Night Watch* was indeed painted by Rembrandt. He allowed for the fact that 'It appears to have been much damaged, but what remains seems to be painted in a poor manner'.

Comparisons of Rembrandt's and Van der Helst's masterpieces continued into the nineteenth century, and were even facilitated from 1817 onwards by the juxtaposition of the two works in the Trippenhuis. In 1828, the painter and future first Director of the National Gallery in London, Sir Charles Eastlake, found it there, apparently in a better state than some fifty years earlier, when Reynolds had viewed it. Eastlake wrote, 'Sir Joshua seems to think lightly of the great picture by Rembrandt, with portraits of the Arquebusiers. I confess I prefer it to all the Van der Helsts, fine as they are. Nothing can be more sunny than this picture'.

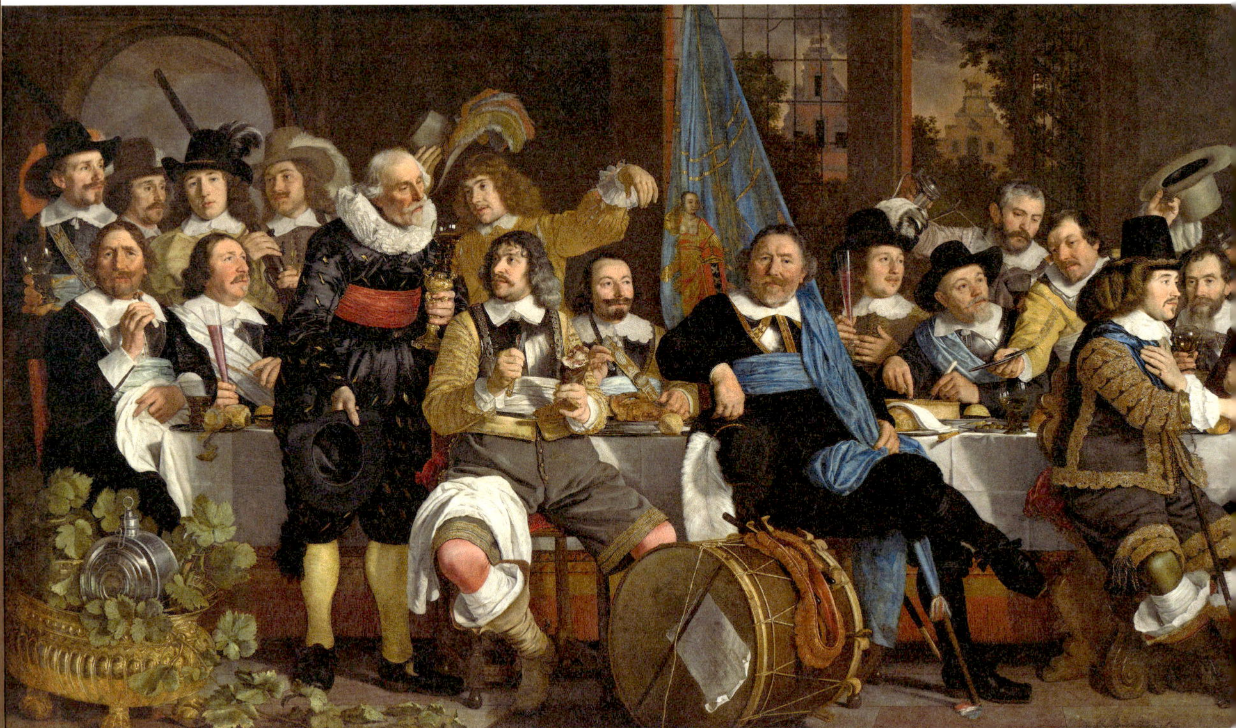

**34**
Bartholomeus van der Helst, *Banquet of the Officers and Other Civic Guardsmen of District XVII in Amsterdam, under the Command of Captain Cornelis Jansz Witsen and Lieutenant Joan Oetgens van Waveren, in Celebration of the Peace of Münster, 10 June 1648*, c. 1648–1650. Oil on canvas, 232 × 547 cm. Amsterdam, Rijksmuseum, inv. no. SK-C-2; on loan from the City of Amsterdam

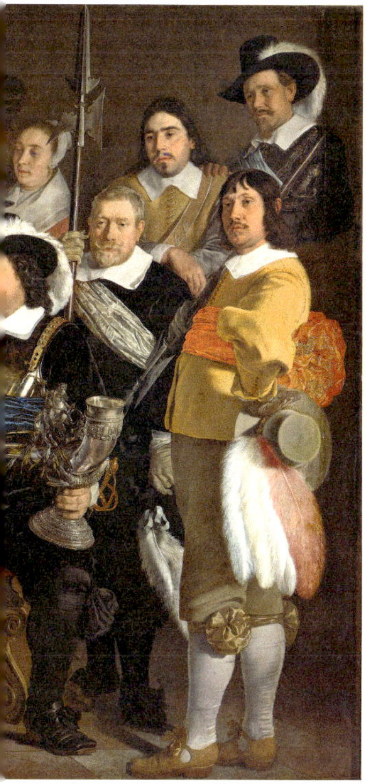

Eastlake's judgement became the prevalent one in the nineteenth century. The renowned French critic, Théophile Thoré, who owes his fame primarily to his 'rediscovery' of Johannes Vermeer, wrote in 1858 that the two works were still vying with one another for the top rung on the ladder of Dutch art. Every inch of Van der Helst's banqueting scene is painted to perfection, according to Thoré, but the whole does not grip you like the poetic paintwork of the Rembrandt, hanging on the opposite side. Both artists depicted reality, but Rembrandt did so in *The Night Watch* with a 'flash of genius'. Van der Helst's way of seeing, on the other hand, 'is more generalized, even vulgar' and, for this reason, 'it corresponds better to the common sensibilities of the crowd'. This is why the banqueting scene is a universal success, whereas *La Ronde de nuit* is not loved by everyone, 'but those who do love it, adore it'. By 1885 *The Night Watch* emerged from this battle of the masterpieces as the overwhelming victor; it was then, after all, that it was installed as the culmination of the Gallery of Honour, thus becoming the centrepiece of the new Rijksmuseum. Van der Helst's picture was awarded the runner-up prize by being relegated to the side wall to the right of it.

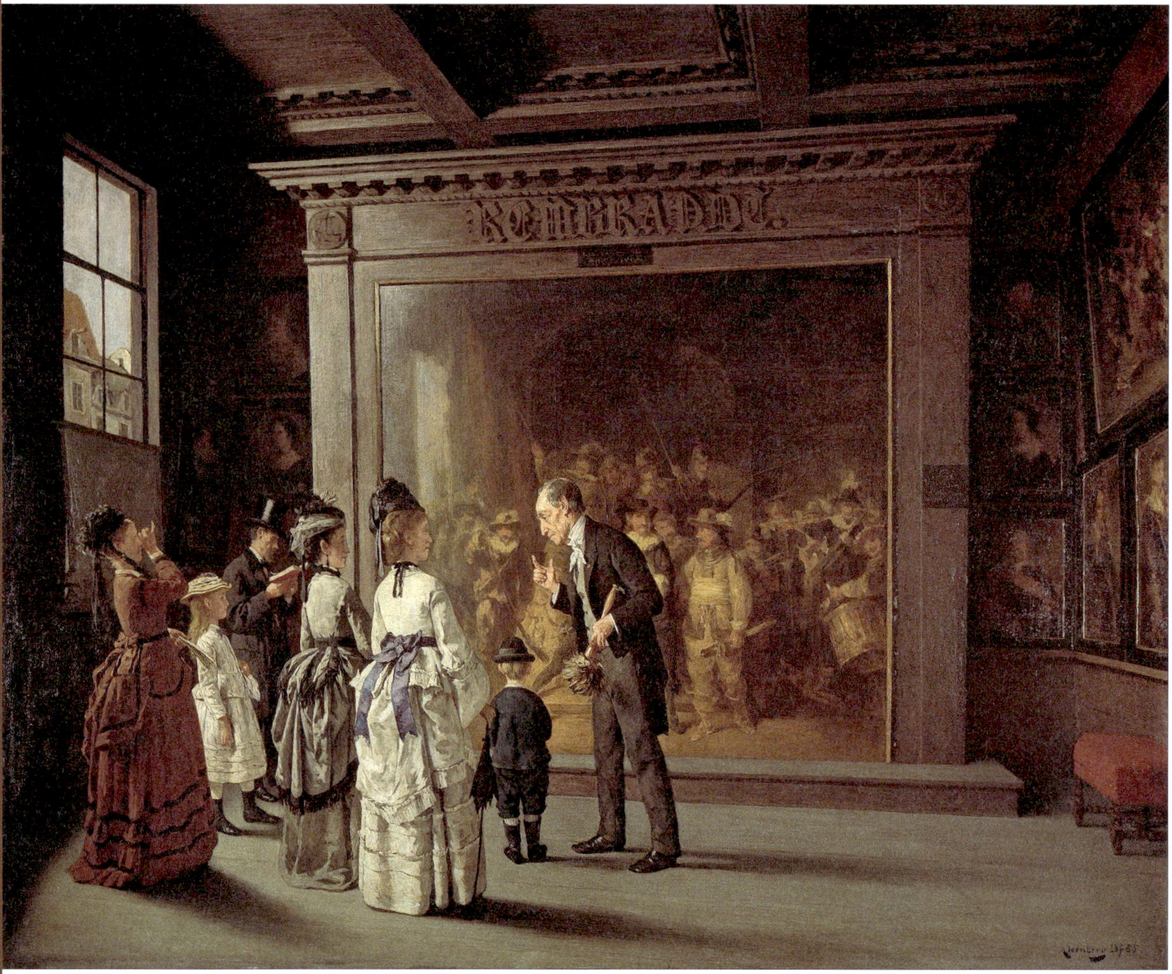


**35**
August Jernberg, *The Night Watch as it hung in the Trippenhuis*, 1880. Malmö, Konstmuseum

## THE NIGHT WATCH ON THE MOVE

One would think that everything would have been done to keep a painting of *The Night Watch*'s size in one place, but, in fact, the opposite has been the case. The enormous canvas has been relocated a total of sixteen times, beginning with the 1715 move from the Kloveniersdoelen to the Amsterdam City Hall on Dam Square. Rembrandt's picture was not the first of the seven works to be removed from its original location in the great hall. That distinction fell to Van der Helst's painting at the end of the seventeenth century. In 1808, during the French occupation of the Dutch Republic, the City Hall became the royal palace of Napoléon Bonaparte's brother Louis. The municipal government transferred a number of works, including Rembrandt's civic guard piece, to the Trippenhuis on Kloveniersburgwal, which had been built in the seventeenth century as the city palace of the fabulously rich Trip family. Almost immediately, however, King Louis demanded its return to his palace. In 1817, four years after the French had departed and the Kingdom of the Netherlands was called into existence, the picture was once again moved to the Trippenhuis [FIG. 35], which became the new home of the Rijks Museum (as the museum's name was spelt at the time). There it remained until the present-day Rijksmuseum opened its doors in 1885.

Disgruntled critics soon began to complain about its location on the central wall in the space at the end of the Gallery of Honour, not because it was considered to lack the requisite stature for such a prominent position, but because the lighting by way of the skylight in the centre of the room was found to be wanting. One of the detractors was the septuagenarian artist Jozef Israëls, who, in 1898, described the Rijksmuseum's Night Watch Gallery as a 'grim grey space' that 'was killing to the painting'. The loan of the painting in the same year to a Rembrandt exhibition just down the road in the newly built Stedelijk Museum, the only exhibition to which *The Night Watch* has ever been lent, added fuel to the fire. In the Stedelijk Museum, the picture hung, as it had in the Trippenhuis, to the right of a large window. It was mounted to celebrate the crowning of Queen Wilhelmina and has the distinction of being the first ever monographic exhibition in the Netherlands.

The debate on how the painting should be lit flared up again as soon as it was returned to its original place in the Rijksmuseum. A committee was formed to deal with the question and it was decided to build an extension behind the Night Watch Gallery where the painting could be hung next to a large window with the light coming from the left [FIG. 36]. That this arrangement did not correspond to the work's original placement was of no concern because it was not known at the time where *The Night Watch* had hung in the great hall of the Kloveniersdoelen. Nonetheless, this new location quickly proved to be unsatisfactory as it was very cramped and only lasted from 1906 to 1925, whereupon the picture was returned to the Night Watch Gallery, but placed on the north-west side wall – that is, the same wall as in the extension – instead of the central wall facing the Gallery of Honour [FIG. 37]. Here it remained until the Second World War.

During the war, *The Night Watch* was placed for safekeeping at no fewer than four different locations. Just before the outbreak of hostilities, it was first transported upright on its stretcher to a depot in Medemblik, a small town on Lake IJssel. A short time later, it was moved with great haste to a bomb shelter in the town of Castricum, on the other side of the peninsular Province of North Holland. There, in order to fit it through the door, it was fortunately not cut down again, but rather removed from its stretcher on the dunes outside and rolled onto a wooden cylinder [FIG. 38]. It remained rolled up for the rest of the war, and was moved twice more, first to a bunker in Heemskerk, about 6 kilometres beneath Castricum, and finally, in March 1942, to the grottoes of Mount Saint Peter near Maastricht, in the south of the country.

In June 1945, after the war had ended, *The Night Watch* finally returned by boat to the Rijksmuseum. It was unrolled and hung in its original honorary position as the triumphant culmination of the Gallery of Honour [FIGS. 40A, B]. Between 1960 and 1984 it was mounted once again on the north-west wall of the room. The last move of significant duration took place during the renovation of the Rijksmuseum from 2003 to 2013. On this and earlier occasions the painting was passed through the slot that had been made in the Night Watch Gallery's floor in 1934. This slot is visible in the ceiling of the passageway that runs through the museum [FIG. 39] and, of course, in the floor itself.

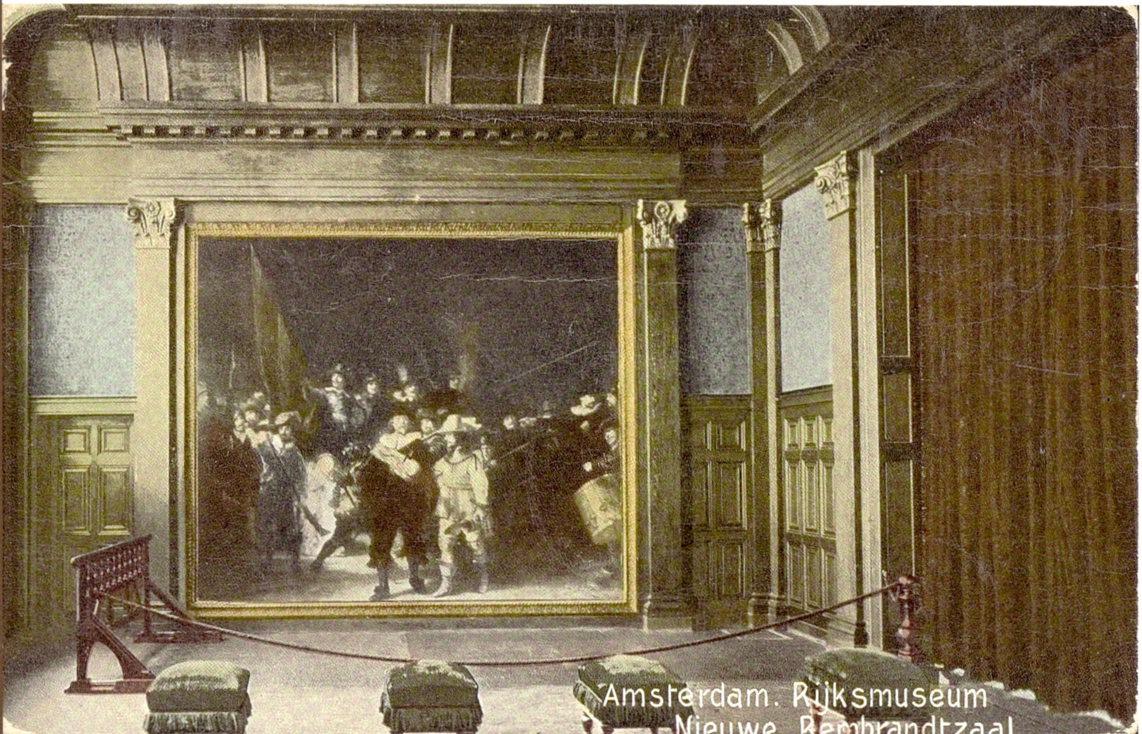


**36**
Postcard of *The Night Watch* in the extension behind the Night Watch Gallery, 1906–1925.
Amsterdam City Archives, inv. no. ANWU01762000003

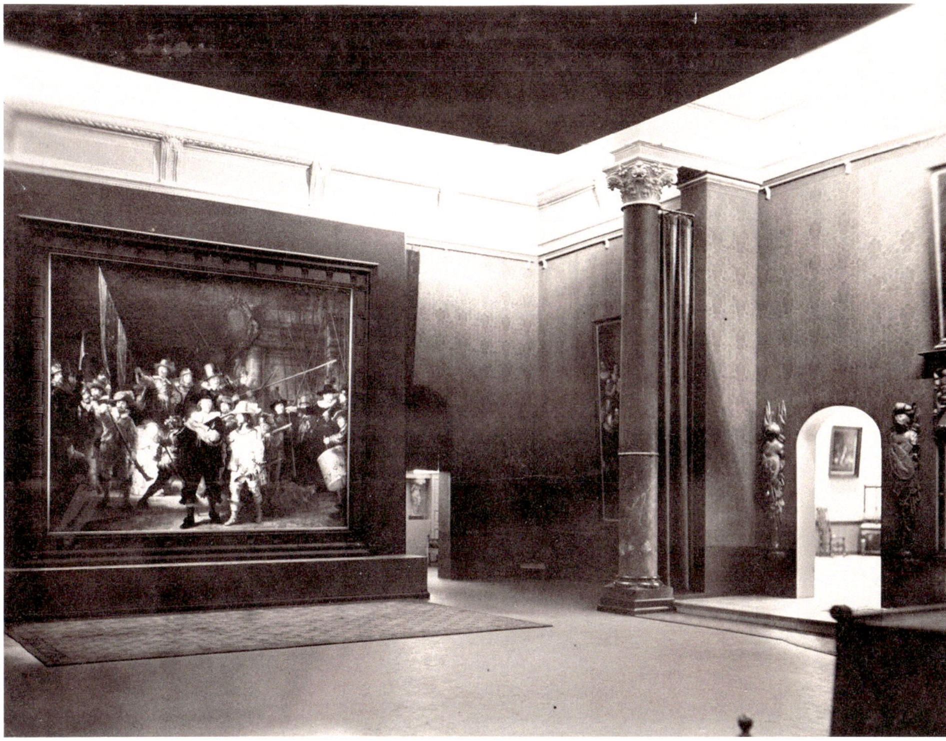

**37**
*The Night Watch* back in the original Night Watch Gallery, 1925–1940. Amsterdam City Archives, inv. no. 010003016369

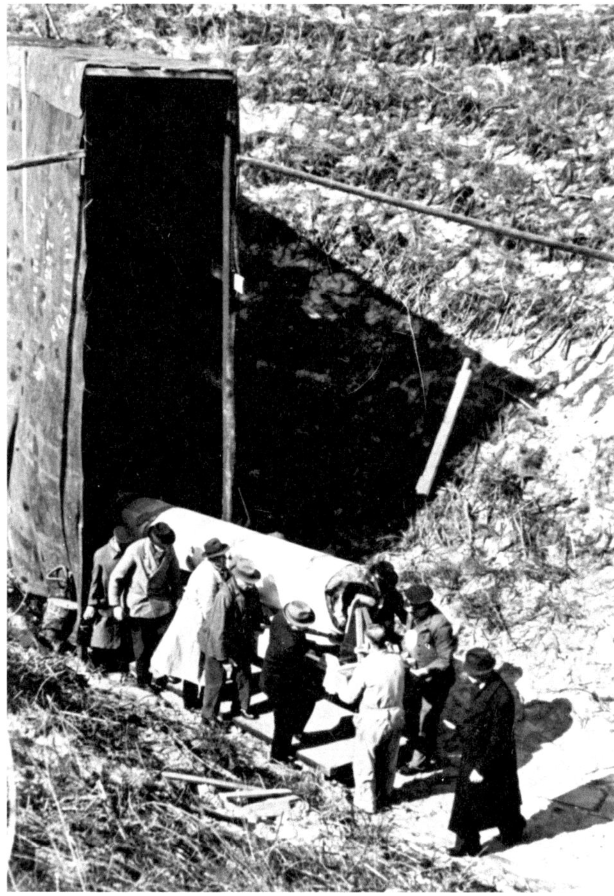

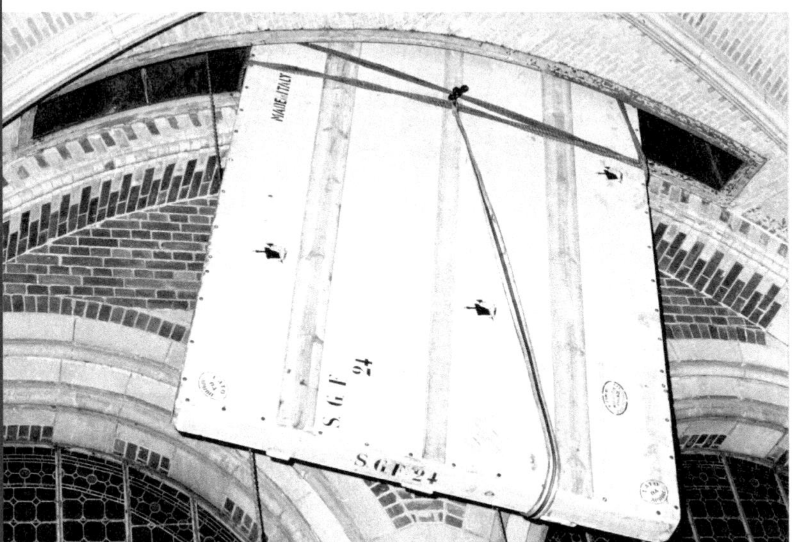

**38**
Rolled onto a wooden cylinder, *The Night Watch* is transported into a bomb shelter, c. 1940. Amsterdam, Rijksmuseum, inv. no. RMA-SSA-F-05307-1

**39**
Painting (not *The Night Watch*) being lowered through the slot in the passageway. Amsterdam, Rijksmuseum, inv. no. HA-0009939

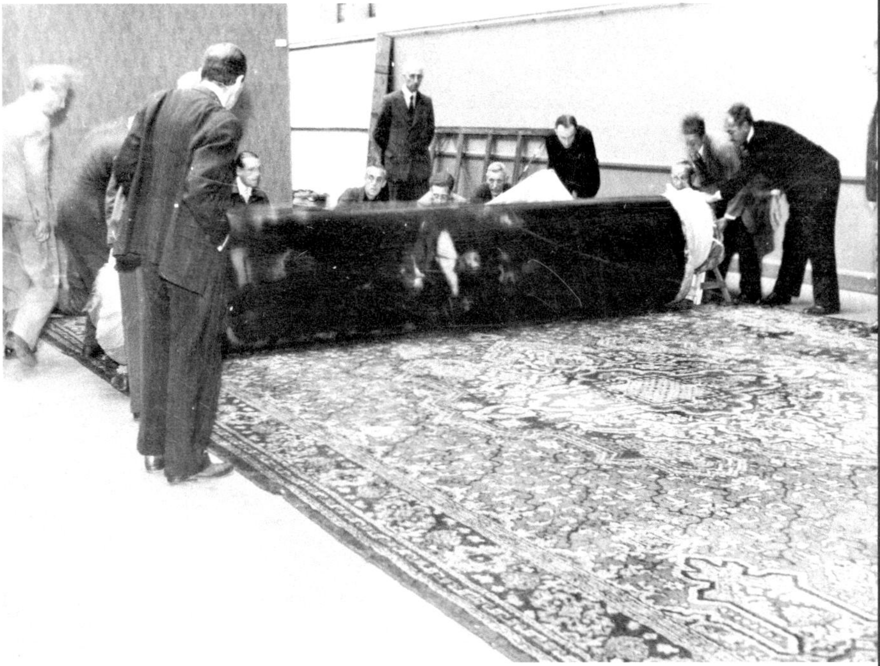

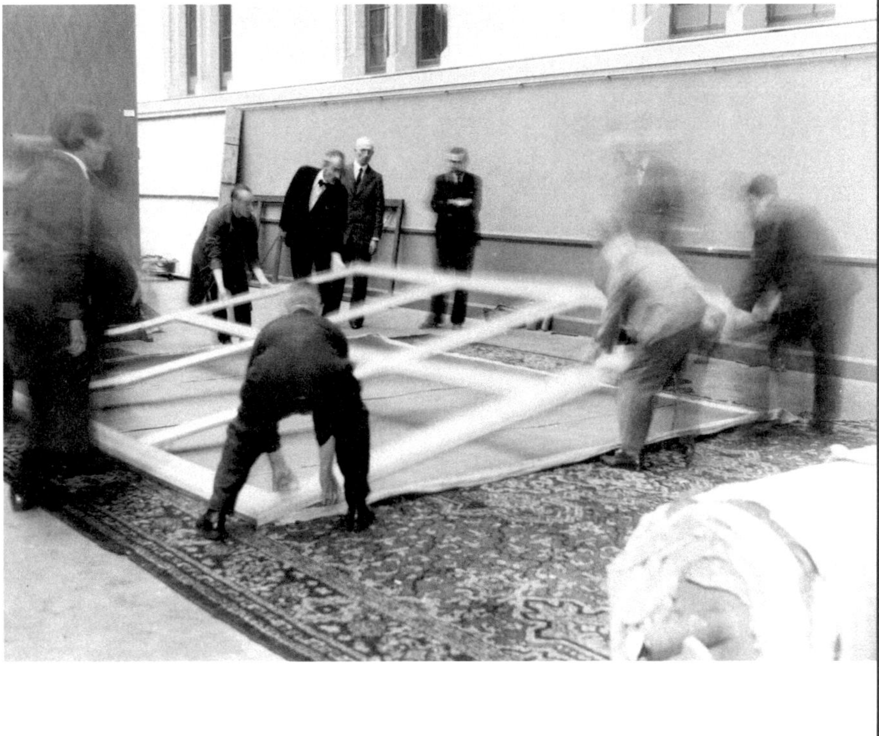

**40A, B**
The return of *The Nightwatch* in the Rijksmuseum after World War II.
Amsterdam, Rijksmuseum; inv. nos. RMA-SSA-F-05415-1, RMA-SSA-F-05388-1

## PREVIOUS RESTORATIONS

*The Night Watch* has certainly had a lot to endure. The Kloveniersdoelen where it first hung was the opposite of a museum environment. From the last quarter of the seventeenth century, it was an inn of some size, where climate fluctuations, smoke from the fireplaces and tobacco pipes, vapours from food and alcohol were the order of the day, and where rowdy guests had few qualms about brushing up against the pictures or even putting an elbow through them. *The Night Watch* was probably one of the canvases that the city paid to have its holes mended in 1698. Was one of these the hole in the drum that until recently had a patch of indeterminate age, or was that one made by the joiner's hammer that was accidentally dropped on the painting in the 1840s? Unfortunately, the picture also has a history of knife incidents. In 1911, a naval cook whose application to rejoin the military was denied took out his anger at the state by striking the canvas with his cobbler's knife. This only damaged the varnish layer, but the consequences of another attack made with a table knife by a mentally ill and unemployed school teacher in 1975 were far greater. The twelve cuts, varying in length from 39 to 100 centimetres, went through the canvas and several also through the lining canvas [FIG. 41]. The perpetrator began at the lower half of Banninck Cocq's figure, even slashing a complete triangular piece out of the painting here, and moved towards the right, ending at the drum. It was, of course, the painting's fame that made it the object of these attacks, as well as a 1990 incident in which it was sprayed with acid.

Another consequence of its renown – indeed of all well-known paintings – has been the numerous treatments *The Night Watch* has been subjected to. In total, there have been 31 documented treatments, including campaigns involving groups of paintings to which Rembrandt's probably belonged. Among these restorations were the many varnish regenerations performed between 1889 and 1936. Known as the Pettenkofer method, after its inventor the chemist Max von Pettenkofer, it entailed exposing the painting to alcohol vapour for some time in an enclosed wooden box. This caused the varnish to soften and swell, thereby closing the minuscule cracks in its surface and making it translucent once again. But this cure was only temporary and the intervals between the treatments became increasingly short. Because of this, and the fact that the brown discolouration remained, it was finally concluded in 1936 that the varnish had to be removed and replaced, which in the end happened after the war.

In at least four restorations a second canvas was adhered to the original to strengthen it. Three of these so-called linings – in 1851, 1945 and 1975 – were affixed using the 'Dutch Method', which had been invented by the Dutch restorer Nicolaas Hopman. This was carried out with wax resin, the first layer of which was applied directly to the back of the original canvas and was then ironed in. Next, the lining canvas was placed and a second layer of wax resin was ironed in. The heat and the pressure from the iron could, of course, result in the flattening of the thick paint, known as *impasto*, on the painting's surface. Fortunately, this was not the case with *The Night Watch*, but the method is no longer used because of the risks involved.

## OPERATION NIGHT WATCH: HOW THE NIGHT WATCH WAS MADE

In 2019 the Rijksmuseum launched Operation Night Watch, a highly ambitious project to research and preserve Rembrandt's gigantic painting. The biggest conservation endeavour not only in the history of the painting, but also in the history of the Rijksmuseum, it involves a multidisciplinary team of more than thirty people: conservators, scientists, curators, data analysists, photographers and general staff, among others. The work is carried out behind a glass wall in front of the public [FIG. 42]. More than thirty different research techniques were employed to study the painting, including a variety of state-of-the-art imaging technologies. For example, macro X-ray fluorescence imaging spectroscopy (MA-XRF) detects chemical elements, on the basis of which it is possible to determine which pigments are present. Another imaging technology is reflectance imaging spectroscopy (RIS), which NASA has been using since the 1970s to photograph minerals on Mars. In paintings, this technique can identify, for instance, various iron-containing earth pigments and organic lakes, and additionally, it can reveal underdrawings, sketches and compositional changes. MA-XRF and RIS added extra insights to those that had already been discovered with older methods, such as the X-radiographs that were made of parts of the painting back in 1947 and of the entire picture in 1976 (X-radiography

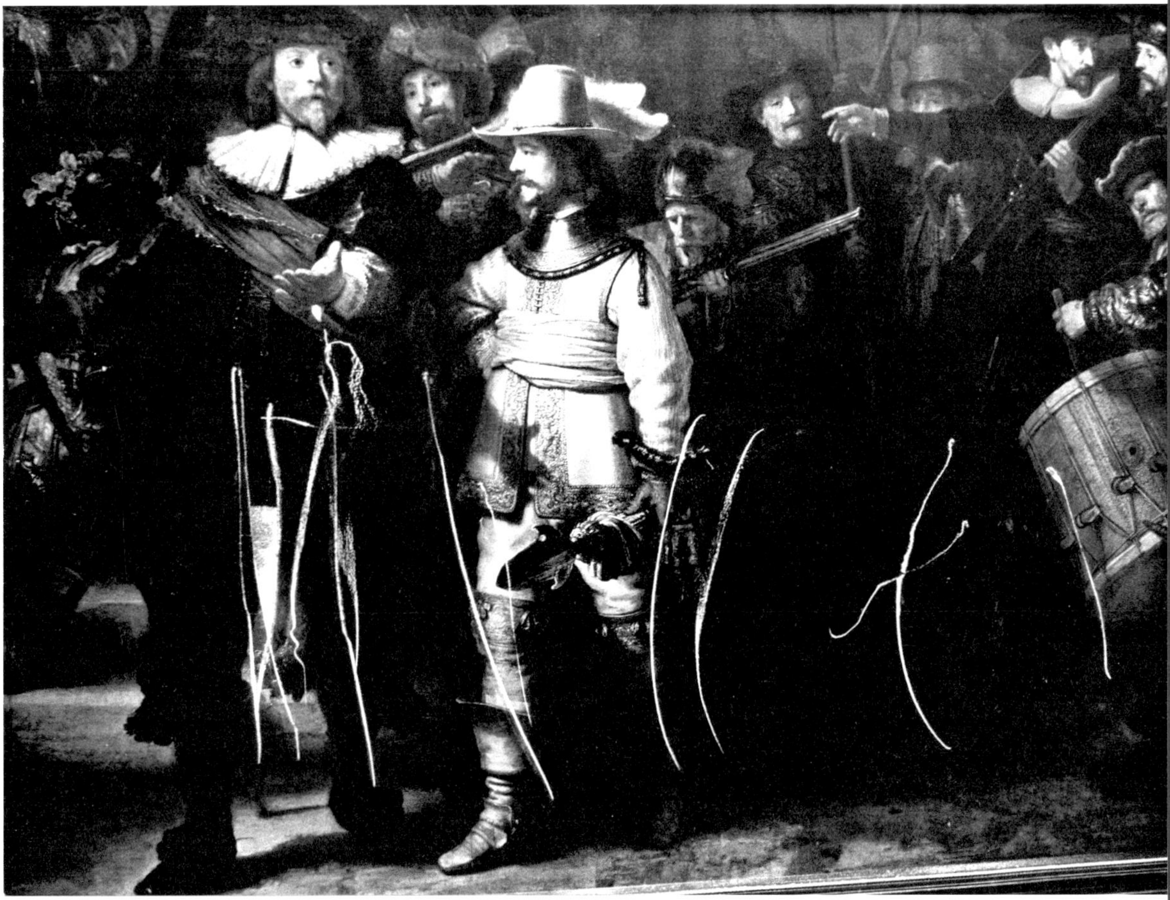

41
The twelve cuts in *The Night Watch*, made during the knife attack on Sunday 14 September 1975. Amsterdam, Rijksmuseum; inv. no. RMA-SSA-F-06510-1-00

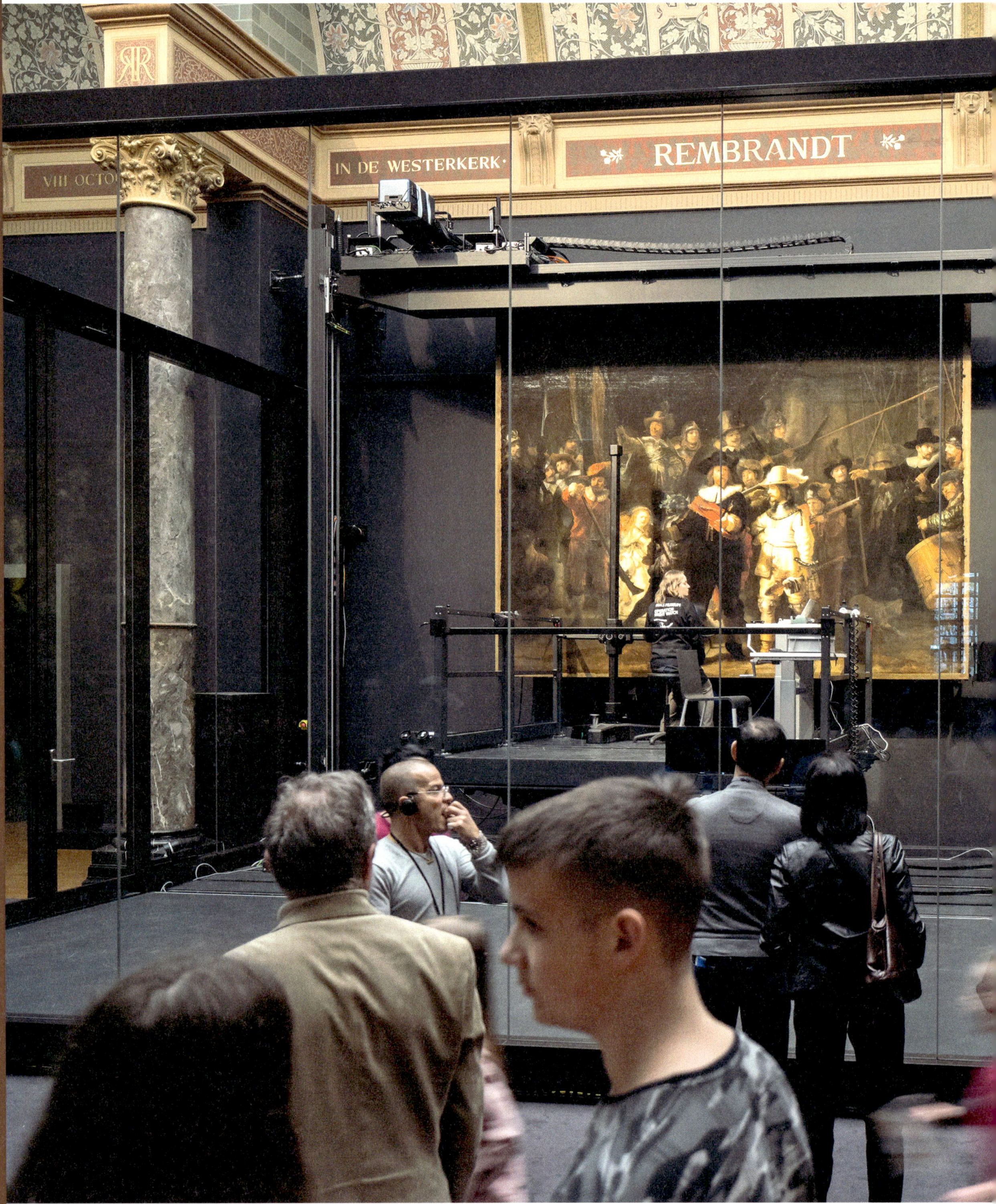
IN DE WESTERKERK·
REMBRANDT

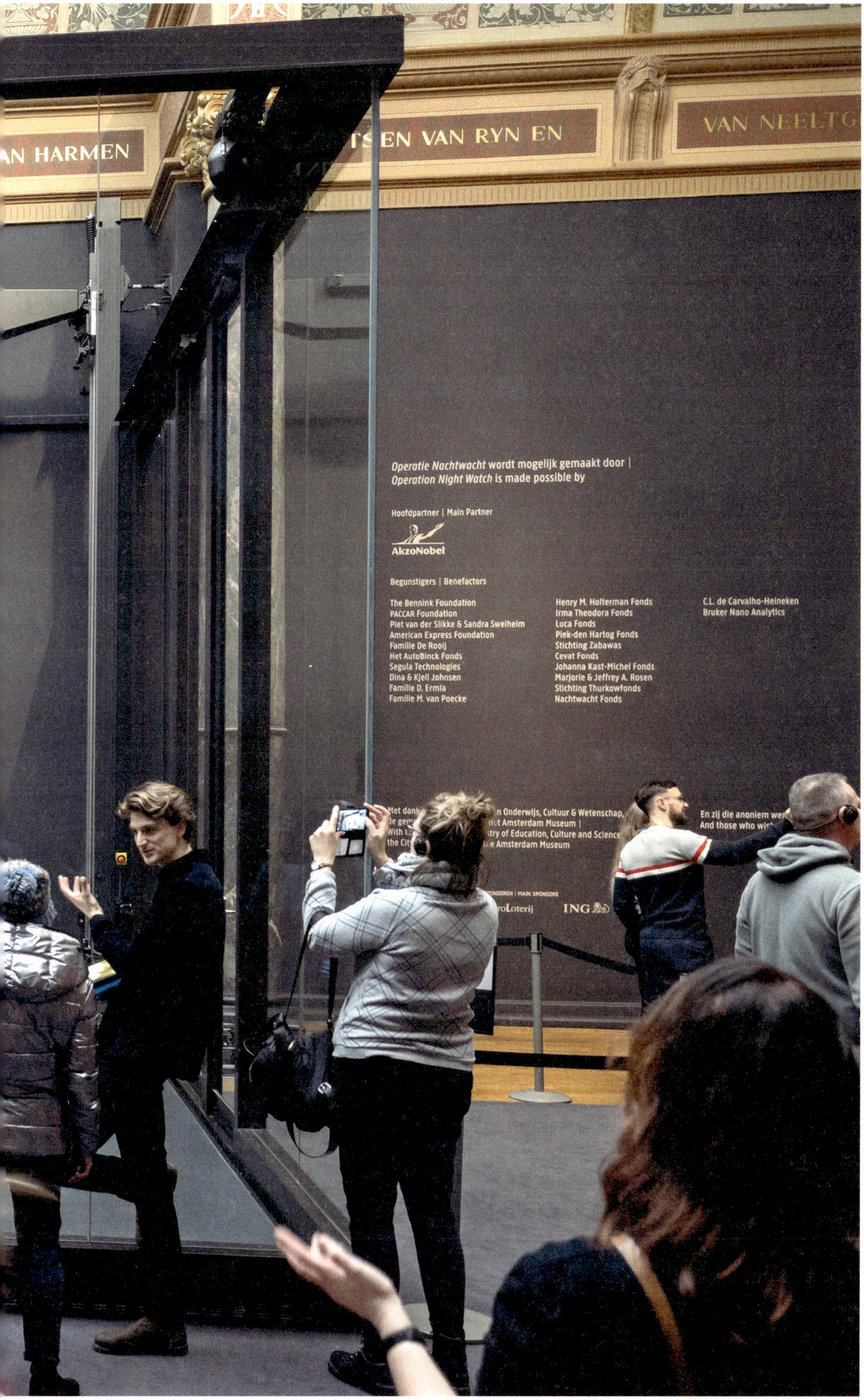


**42**
The glass wall placed in the Night Watch Gallery during Operation Night Watch, 2022

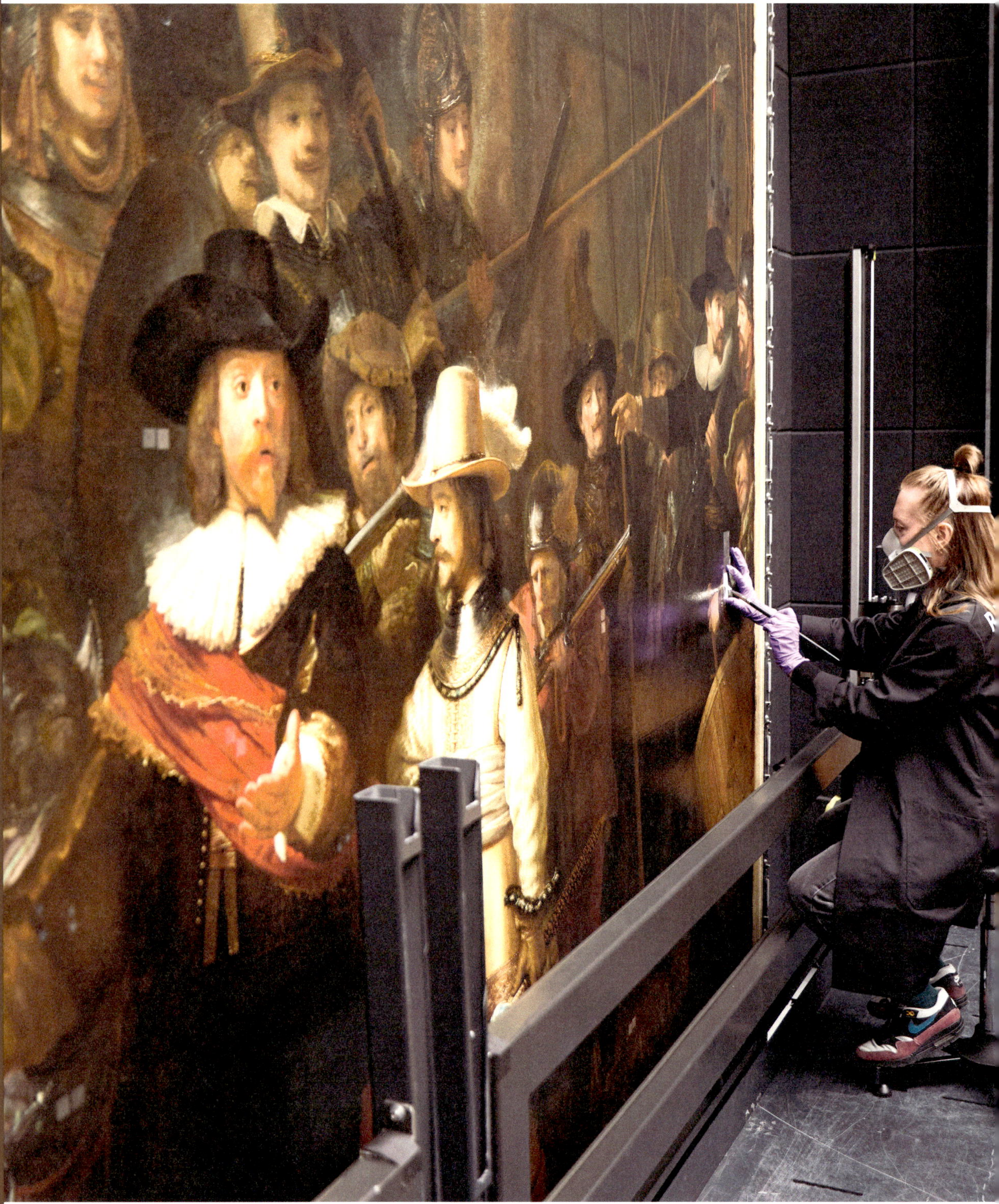

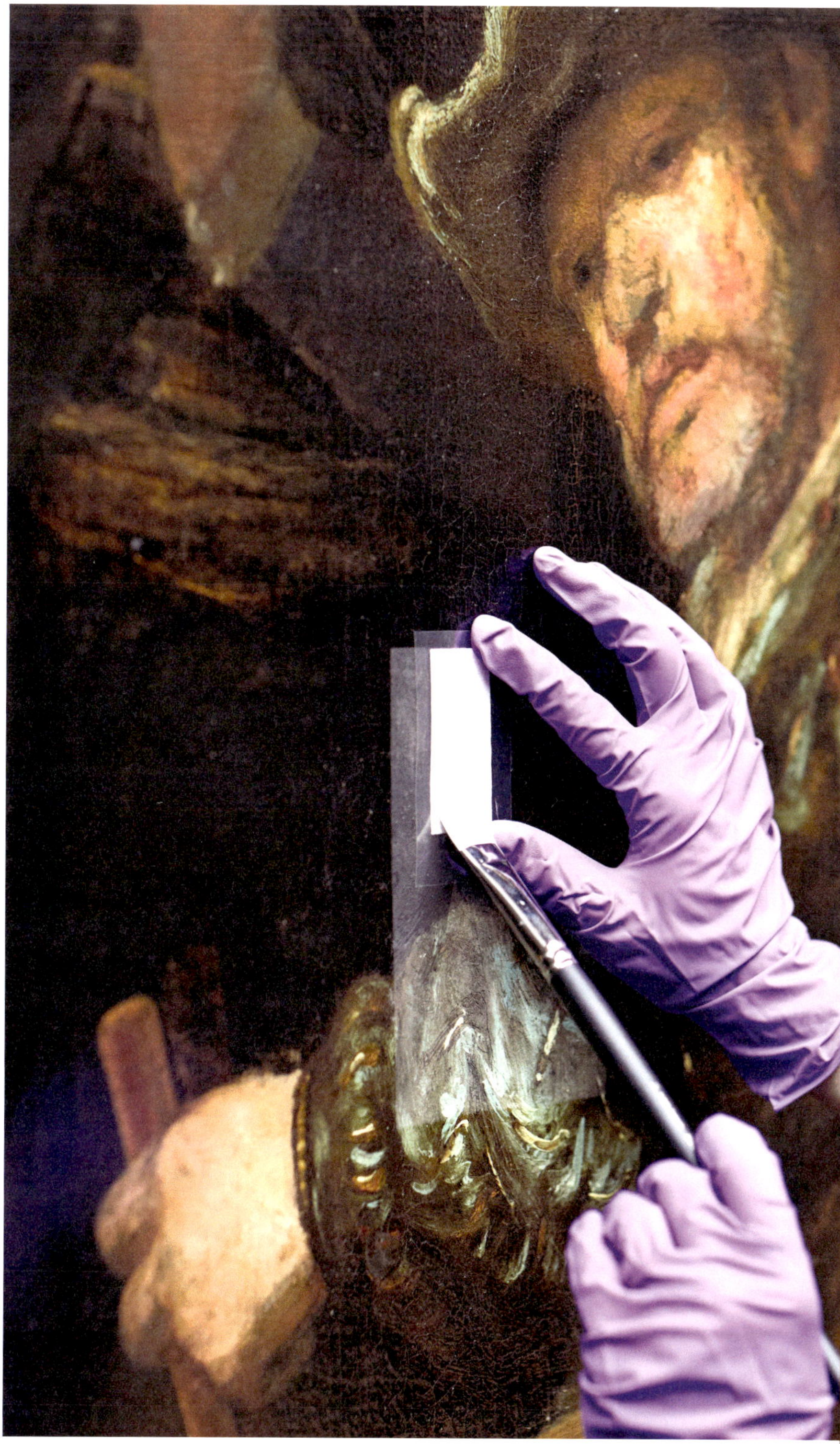

**43**
The old varnish is removed from *The Night Watch*, 2024

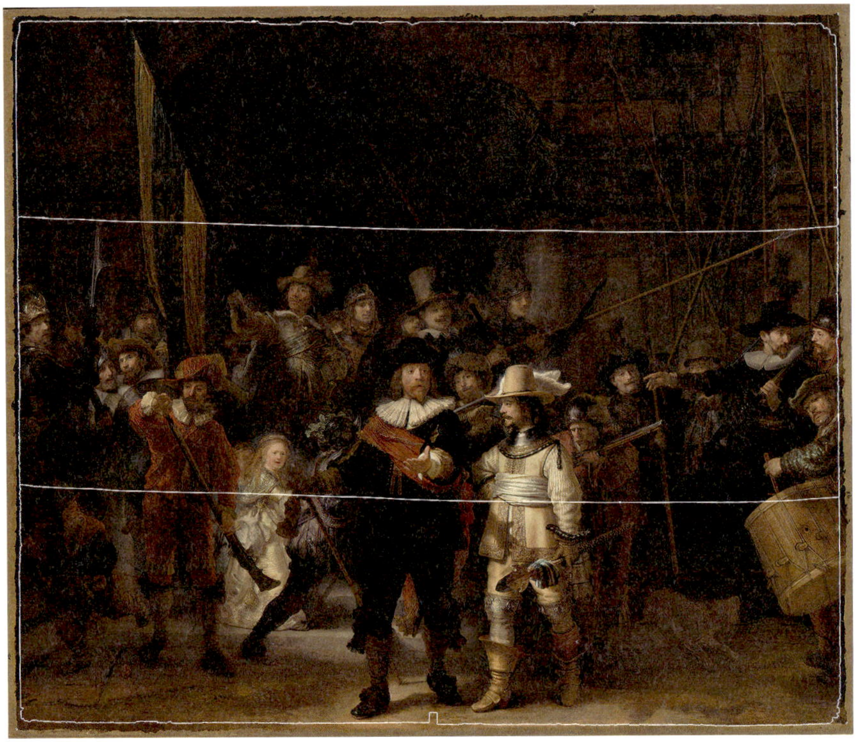

44
*The Night Watch* with lines indicating the horizontal seams of the canvas

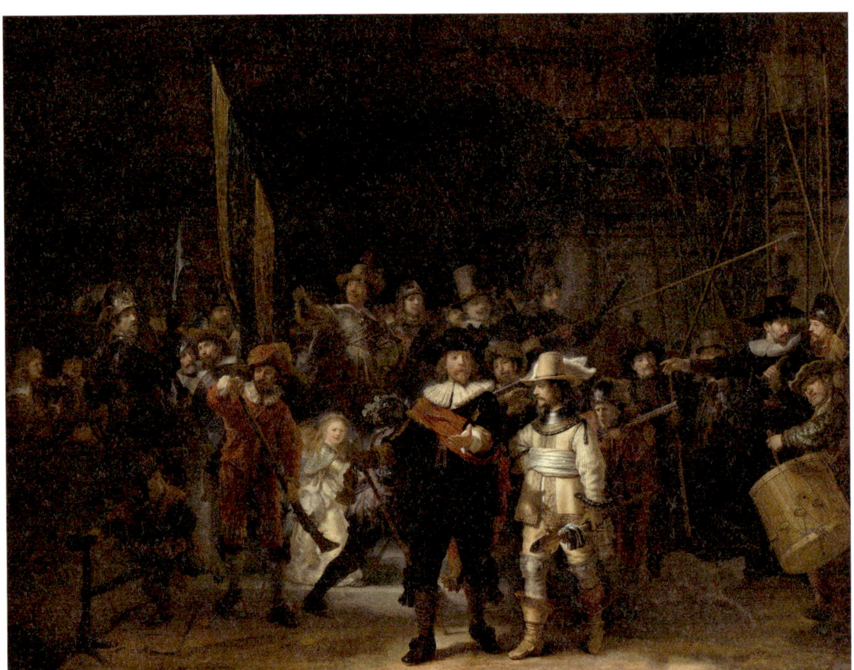

45
*The Night Watch* with the cut off pieces reconstructed

registers heavy elements on and under the surface of a painting, such as lead, which is present, for example, in lead white).

The research phase of the project resulted in numerous new insights into how Rembrandt went about executing what was at the time by far the largest commission he had ever embarked upon. Only *The Conspiracy of the Batavians under Claudius Civilis*, painted for the Amsterdam City Hall between 1661 and 1662, would, at 5.5 × 5.5 metres, surpass it in size. But that work was subsequently reduced to a fragment significantly smaller than the 1642 masterpiece. The first question that arises is, where did Rembrandt execute this enormous work? The wager, mentioned earlier, from which we know exactly when Pickenoy delivered his portrait, also reveals that his painting was not executed on location, which may have been the case for the others as well. However, the hypothesis that Rembrandt painted *The Night Watch* in an open-air gallery behind the house that he purchased in 1639 has not found overwhelming support and the question is still open.

Like every painting, *The Night Watch* began life as a bare support, in its case three horizontal pieces of canvas that were stitched together. The resulting seams are visible approximately halfway up the figure of Captain Banninck Cocq and just below the cartouche carrying the names of the guardsmen [FIG. 44]. The piece of canvas forming the middle of the painting is 140 centimetres wide, which was a standard seventeenth-century loom width. As all three strips were taken from the same bolt of fabric, those at the top and bottom would originally have been 140 centimetres wide as well, but are now approximately 107 and 115.5 centimetres respectively. The total height of the entire canvas available to Rembrandt would have been 420 centimetres, but on the basis of a scale bar found in the underdrawing of a seventeenth-century copy [FIG. 16] it was possible to estimate that the original height of the picture had been 406 centimetres and the original width about 513 centimetres. The painting now measures 362.5 × 436 centimetres. Therefore, it would have been reduced at the top and bottom by approximately 43.5 centimetres and about 77 centimetres on the sides.

It is not known what happened to the missing pieces: were they simply chucked in the bin? A more optimistic scenario would be that an artist or artists active at the time, that is, in or shortly after 1715, used them as the support for new paintings. It is conceivable, therefore, that sometime in the future, MA-XRF imaging of these works may uncover bits of *The Night Watch*. In the meantime, a neural network was trained to compare every millimetre of the original with the copy, which, because it was not painted by Rembrandt himself and is significantly smaller, has a somewhat different look. After the computer had learnt how the probable copyist, Gerrit Lundens, had transformed the still existing part of *The Night Watch* into his much-reduced version, the neural network was taught to reverse the process in order to recreate the parts of the original that had been removed [FIG. 45].

Before the paint can be applied, it is necessary to prepare the canvas. Most seventeenth-century Dutch canvases were first given an isolation layer of glue sizing. However, no indication of such a layer could be found in any of the paint samples taken from *The Night Watch*. Instead, Rembrandt impregnated the surface of the canvas with a lead-containing oil. The broad sweeps of the brush used to apply this layer are very apparent in the MA-XRF lead distribution map [FIG. 46]. There is a distinct possibility that the painting's location on the potentially damp outer wall of the great hall of the Kloveniersdoelen was taken into account when the decision was made to deviate in this way from the standard practice. An early seventeenth-century manuscript on painting techniques gives an example of how paint had separated from a glue-sized canvas after being hung on a damp wall for several years, and recommends the use of lead-rich oil as a more satisfactory alternative.

After impregnating the canvas with lead-containing oil, Rembrandt applied a preparatory underlayer over the entire surface. Known simply as the ground, such priming layers were also standard procedure, but here too the young Dutch artist proved himself to be an innovator. For the first time in his career, he made use of a so-called quartz ground, a natural earth layer remarkably rich in quartz and with a high amount of clay minerals [FIG. 47]. This became a hallmark of his and his workshop's paintings: more than 45 paintings on canvas executed by Rembrandt and his circle investigated to date contain this kind of ground, and it has not been found in any works by other artists. The quartz ground would have been an economical solution for a painting the size of *The Night Watch*, as only one layer was needed and the main ingredient river clay was cheap. The quartz ground had another advantage: canvases to which it was applied could be rolled up more easily and moved from place to place. This may, therefore, be an additional argument for *The Night Watch* not being executed in the great hall of the Kloveniersdoelen. Rembrandt deliberately left the brown quartz ground layer exposed here and there in the painting, using it as a middle tone. The sword held by *rondassier* Claes van Cruysbergen (no. 18), who stands to the right of the standard bearer, is an example of this [FIG. 48]. Another interesting example is Sergeant Rombout Kemp's extended right hand, the remarkably unfinished appearance of which is due in part to this use of the ground layer as a middle tone [FIG. 49]. But not everywhere was it intended to be as much in evidence as it now is. Abrasion has caused more of the quartz ground layer to be exposed over time, for example in the dog.

As no preliminary drawings for *The Night Watch* have come down to us, it has long been speculated that Rembrandt made a compositional brush drawing on the canvas itself. Proof for this was finally unearthed as one of the most fascinating discoveries of the Operation Night Watch team: the presence of a light-coloured sketch throughout the painting [FIG. 50]. This compositional sketch was executed with chalk-rich paint and is visible in the MA-XRF calcium map. Such a chalk sketch is impossible to detect with more traditional imaging techniques such as infrared reflectography, which registers pigments containing carbon (mostly black) and X-radiography. That may be one of the reasons why it has never been found previously in Rembrandt's work. The sketch is partly responsible for the ghostly appearance of the dog at the lower right, which, due to abrasion, has become more visible than intended. It has also become exposed in the faces of some of the civic guardsmen. The chalk-rich paint was used to define the forest of pikes on the right side of the composition, too, three of which did not make it into the final composition [FIG. 51]. There is also a second partisan with a long blade present in the MA-XRF calcium map between the figures of Frans Banninck Cocq and Lieutenant Wilhem van Ruytenburch that was subsequently painted out [FIG. 52]. Especially intriguing are the forms Rembrandt sketched in the upper middle of the canvas, inside the arch [FIG. 53]. Some of these shapes might be alternative positions of the company's banner. The squiggly lines on the right of the arch seem to show it wrapped around its pole.

Some pictorial elements were sketched in dark brown. Unlike the light-coloured, chalk-based sketch, such dark brown ones have been found in a number of other paintings by the Dutch master. The position of the feet of Jan Claesen Leijdeckers (no. 24), the musketeer to the right of Wilhem van Ruytenburch, was initially indicated with these dark lines. The final position of the feet was altered, but the sketched-in ones are visible to the naked eye and are very distinct in the RIS image [FIG. 54]. Another instance where a dark sketch was used is the metal collar or gorget of the pikeman directly above Wilhem van Ruytenburch in the picture. The lance held by the civic guardsman next to him was also initially sketched in dark paint.

Once the initial composition had been established, the individual civic guardsman would have sat for Rembrandt one by one. No separate drawings of these sitters exist, which suggests that Rembrandt painted them directly on the canvas. This appears to have been a standard procedure among seventeenth-century Dutch portraitists. Portrait drawings by Frans Hals, Michiel van Mierevelt and Bartholomeus van der Helst – to name only a few of Rembrandt's more prominent colleagues in this genre – have not come down to us, and the small number that he himself made were most likely done to show the patron a change of composition he was contemplating. How many times and for how long the eighteen guardsmen would have had to pose for the master is not known, but they probably did not have to hang about for the artist to complete every last detail of their likeness. For example, if they were depicted wearing their own clothing, they would have left this in the workshop to be placed on a wooden or linen lay figure.

Dozens of the small changes Rembrandt made to the composition of *The Night Watch* had already been discovered in the past by close comparison of the X-radiographs with the picture itself. For example, the blade of the partisan held by Van Ruytenburch was enlarged twice, probably as the result of Rembrandt's concern that the diagonals in the picture produce the desired effect [FIGS. 55, 56]. A number of other changes were discovered by the Operation Night Watch team using the MA-XRF scanner. For example, brightly coloured feathers once adorned the helmet of Claes van Cruysbergen (no. 18), the *rondassier* next to the standard bearer. From the iron, copper and mercury maps we know that these feathers must have been composed of yellow earth, azurite and vermilion. Rembrandt later painted them out [FIG. 57].

The Operation Night Watch team also discovered a new pigment in Rembrandt's palette: an orange

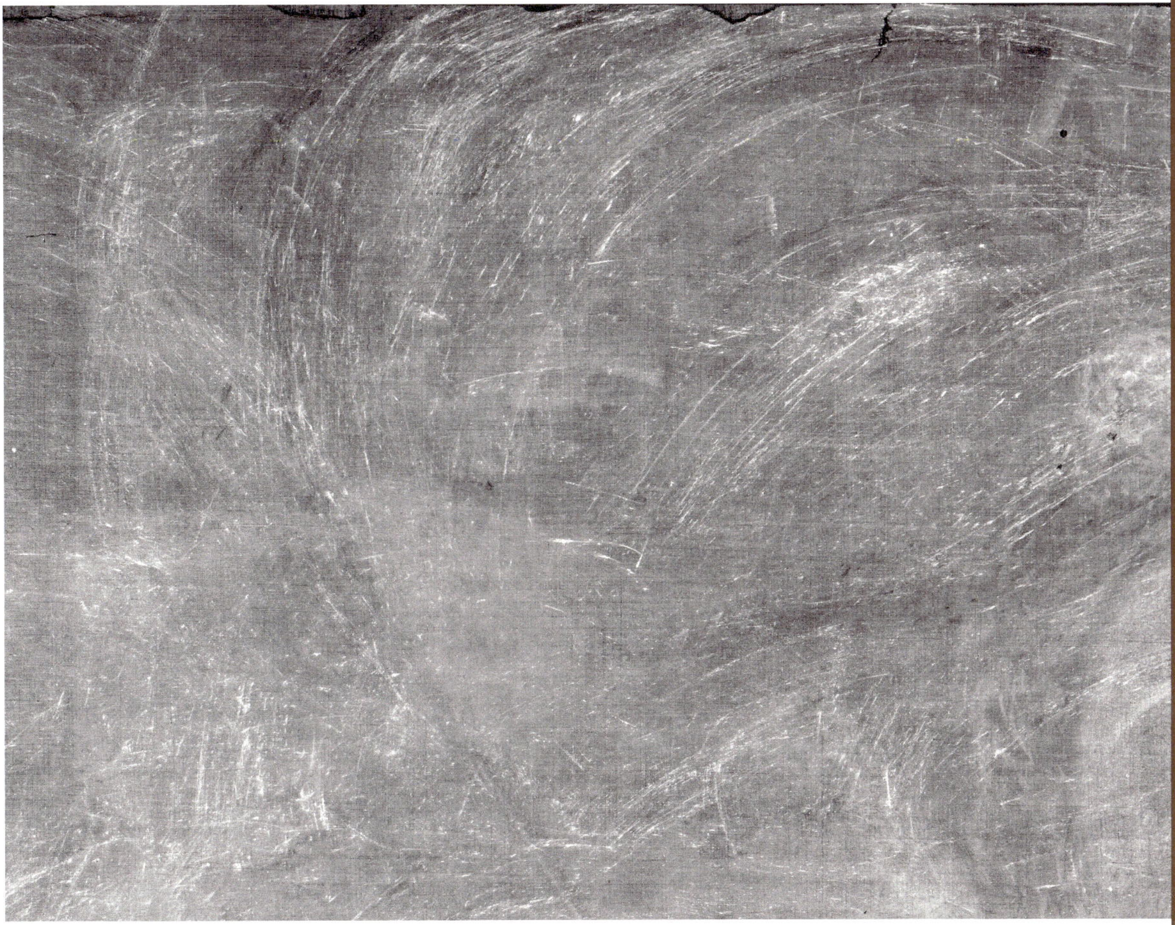

**46**
Detail from the MA-XRF lead distribution map showing the sweeping movements with which the lead-containing oil sizing was applied on the canvas

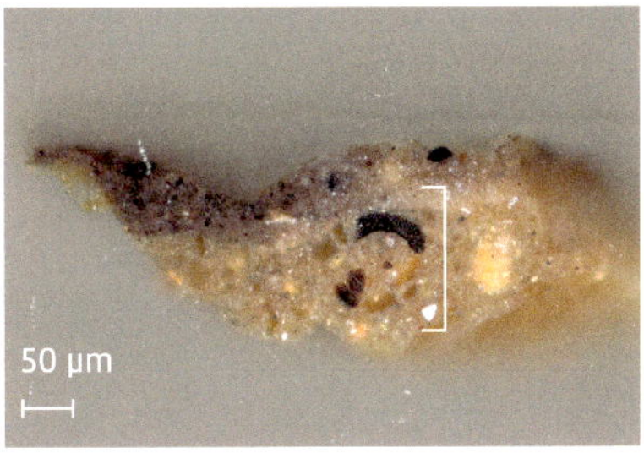


**47**
Paint cross-section taken from the centre of the dark background, left of the lance, showing the quartz ground

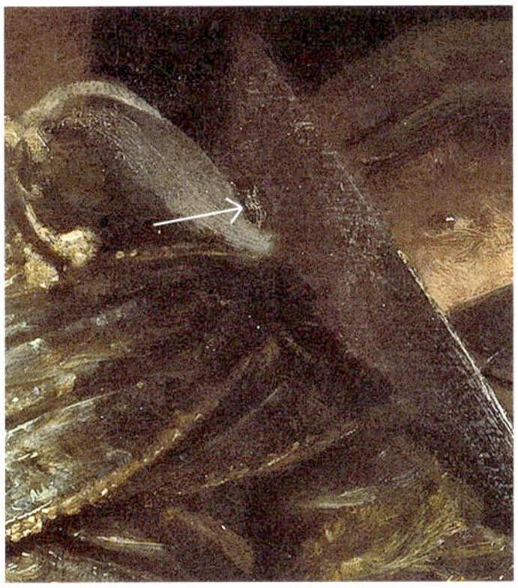

**48**
Detail of the *rondassier*'s sword

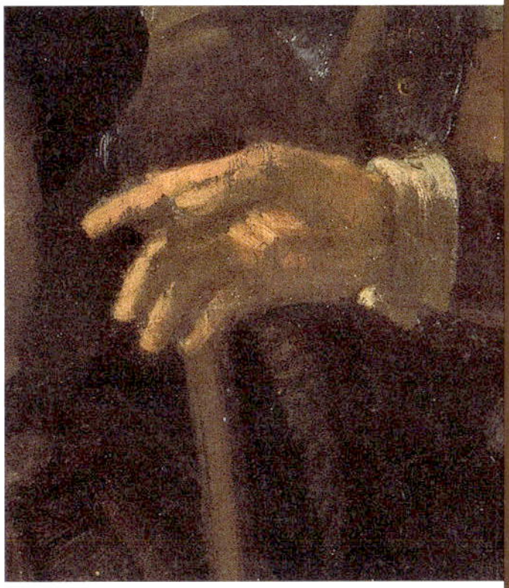

**49**
Detail of Sergeant Rombout Kemp's outstretched hand

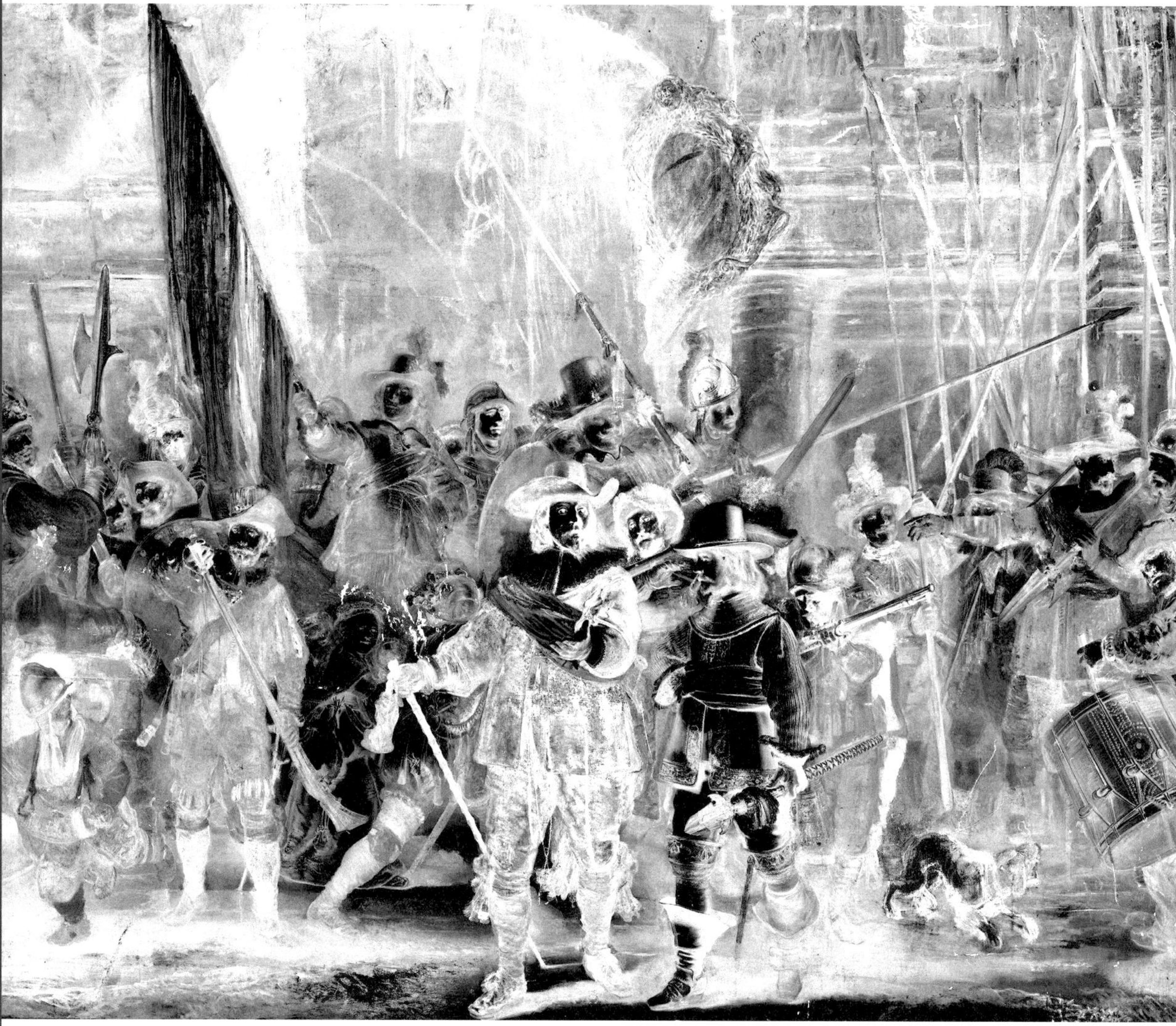

**50**
MA-XRF calcium distribution map of *The Night Watch*, showing the compositional sketch made with a light-coloured chalk-rich paint

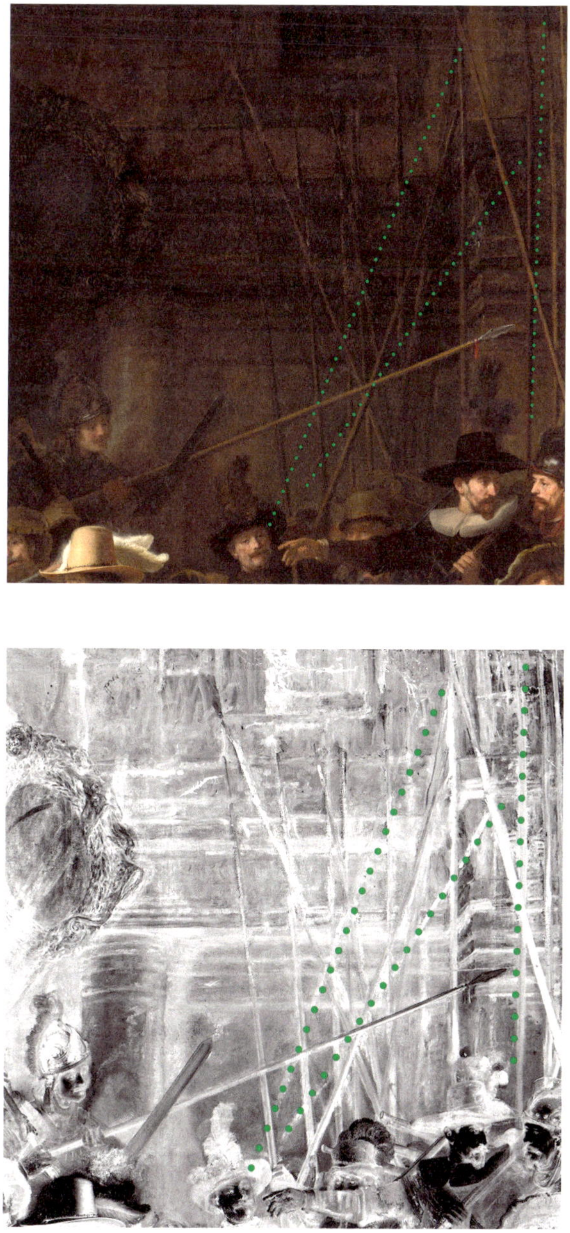

**51**
Detail of the MA-XRF calcium distribution map, showing the pikes on the right side of the composition. On the left the positioning of the three pikes that didn't make it into the final composition can be seen

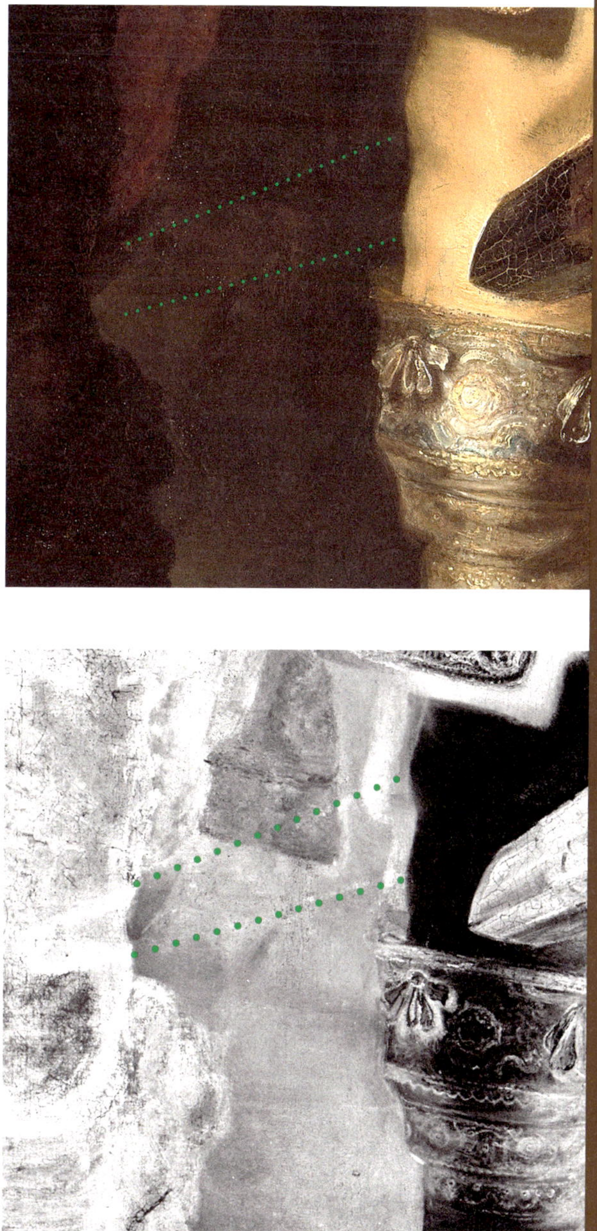

**52**
Detail of the MA-XRF calcium distribution map, showing a second partisan that was painted out at an early stage

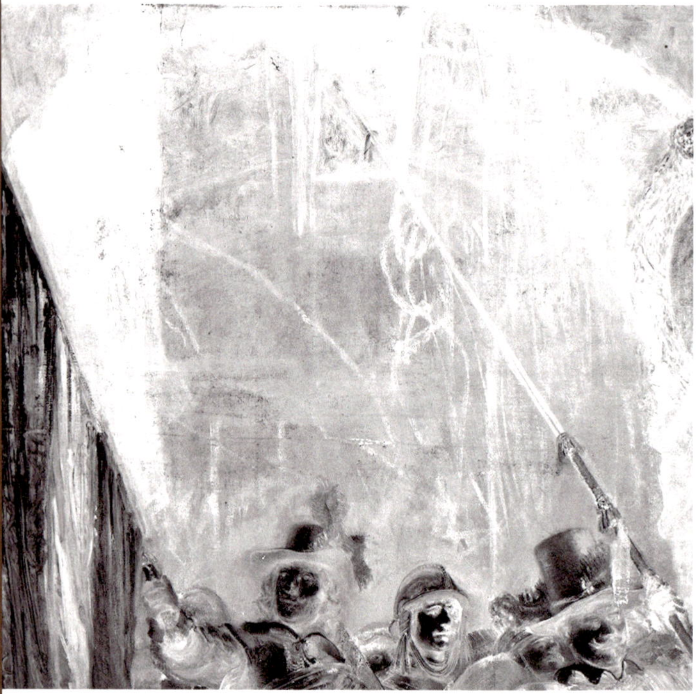

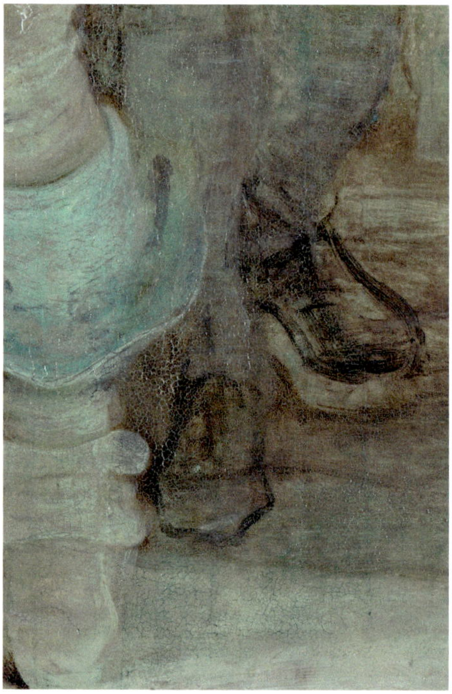

**53**
Detail of the MA-XRF calcium distribution map, possibly showing alternative positions of the company's banner

**54**
Detail of the RIS-SWIR false colour image (2100, 1501, 1099 nm), showing an alternative position of the feet in the dark sketch

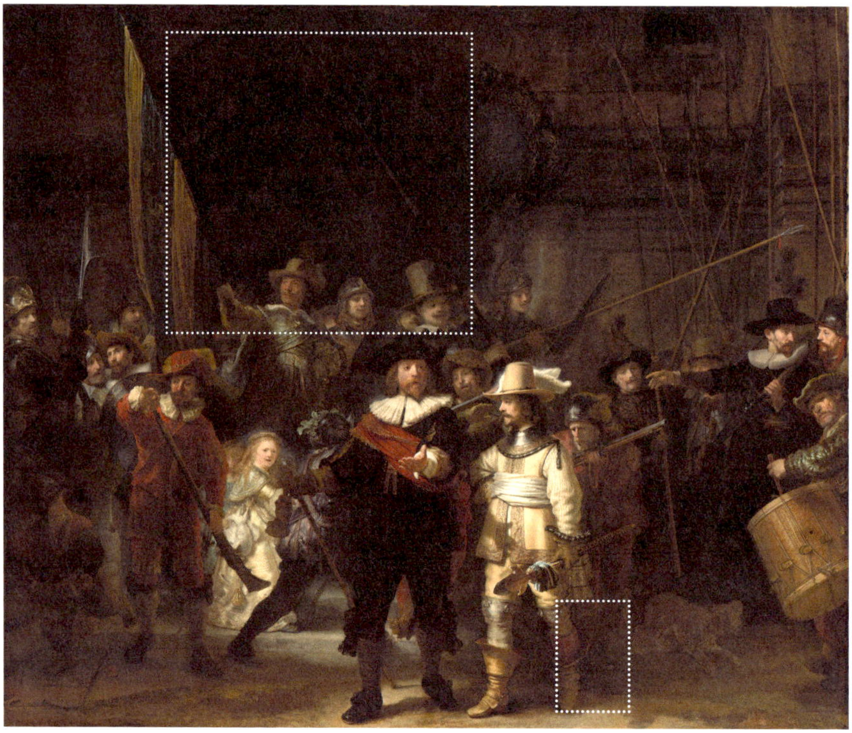

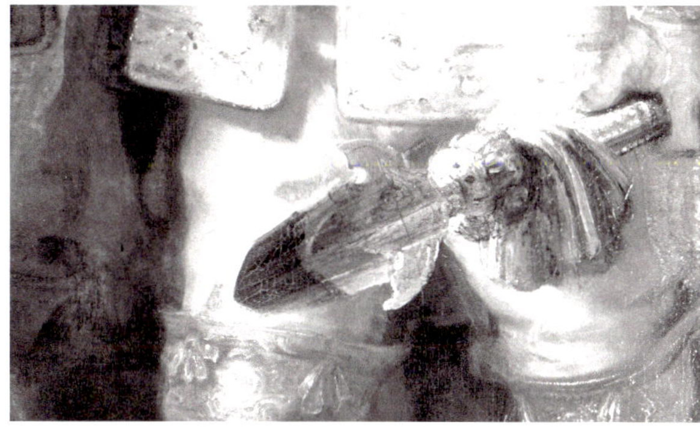

**55**
Detail from the X-radiograph of Lieutenant Wilhem van Ruytenburch's partisan, showing that the length of the blade was altered twice

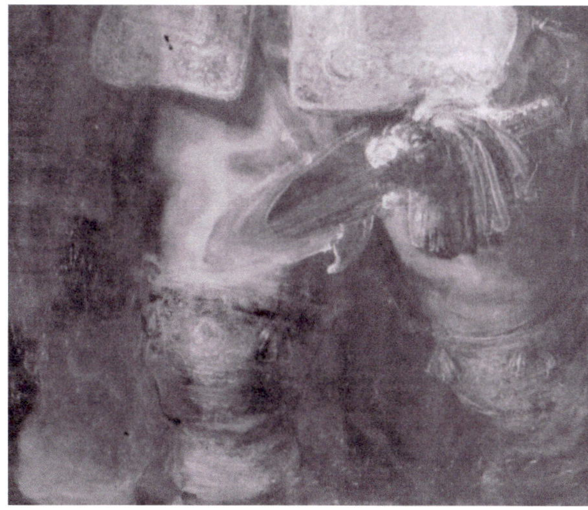

**56**
Detail from the infrared reflectogram of Lieutenant Wilhem van Ruytenburch's partisan, showing that Rembrandt changed it even more than was previously thought on the basis of the X-radiograph

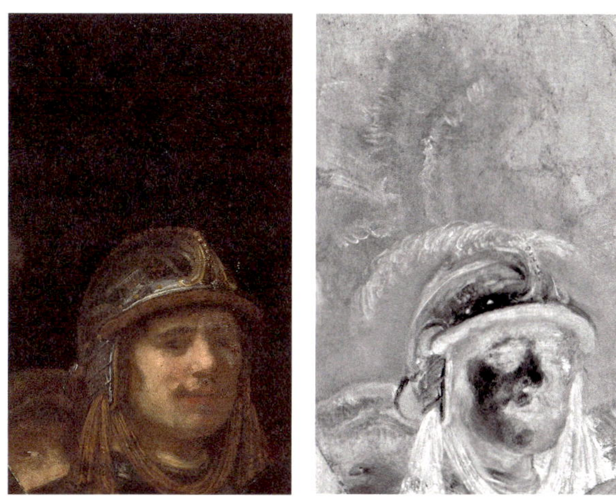

**57**
Detail from the MA-XRF iron distribution map showing the feathers painted with red and yellow earth pigments that initially adorned the helmet of Claes van Cruysbergen

mixture of two arsenic-based pigments, pararealgar and semi-amorphous pararealgar that was primarily used in Dutch still lifes. It was also quite common in Italian painting, but has not been found elsewhere in Rembrandt's oeuvre. These respectively yellow and orange to red pigments were discovered in *The Night Watch* in the gold embroidered Amsterdam coat of arms held by two lions on Lieutenant Van Ruytenburch's buff coat and on his sleeves [FIG. 58].

The thickness of the paint that replicates the three-dimensional form of the embroidery on that coat is one of the most striking features of Rembrandt's technique [FIG. 59]. The eighteenth-century supervisor of the city's art collection, Jan van Dijk, claimed that this part of the picture 'is so high in Paint that one might grate a Nutmeg on it'. This technique of sculpting with paint in order to reconstruct objects three-dimensionally is reminiscent of how fourteenth-century Italian painters moulded gesso (gypsum bound in size) to reproduce textured surfaces, or how Jan and Hubert van Eyck made gilded and painted reliefs using tin moulds, which they attached to the Ghent Altarpiece. Rembrandt's immediate model, however, was probably Jan Lievens, who was already experimenting with such textural tricks in their early days in Leiden. Although Rembrandt himself had employed it earlier, never before had he used it in such a refined manner. The paint surface is actually indented where Banninck Cocq's hand casts its shadow on the coat, and the more intense the highlights, the further the paint soars upwards from the canvas like a miniature mountain range. The light reflected from its peaks and valleys causes the embroidered decorative bands to glitter as much as the gilded halos of the early Renaissance paintings. The effect of such reliefs on the creation of pictorial depth was described as early as the sixteenth century, when the Italian artists' biographer Giorgio Vasari criticized the incorrect use of this method by Bernardino Pinturicchio. The latter had depicted a Roman triumphal arch in the background of a painting, but because the columns were done in low relief, rather than receding they seemed to advance out of the foreground. It is amazing to realize that this little area of very thickly applied paint in *The Night Watch* can create such a powerful illusion of depth in the entire picture.

How exactly Rembrandt got the paint on Van Ruytenburch's buff coat so thick has been one of the greatest mysteries of *The Night Watch*, but the latest round of research has shed new light on this question. It was discovered that the mineral plumbonacrite was present in areas of the painting where lead white impasto was used. This is not an original component of the paint but a chemical degradation product. Its presence may suggest that Rembrandt used an oil medium thickened with lead oxide to create his lead white impasto paints. From all of the above we can conclude that Rembrandt was just as innovative in the use of his materials and his painting techniques as he was in his pictorial means.

## WERE THE THREE PAINTINGS ON THE LONG WALL A COORDINATED EFFORT?

While there can be no doubt that the entire ensemble of seven paintings in the great hall of the Kloveniersdoelen was not conceived according to a predetermined plan, there is still the question of how much coordination was involved in the making of the three works for the long wall in 1642. In terms of the materials, it appears to have been very little. As the widths of the individual strips of canvas vary in each picture, it is certain that they did not all come from the same bolt. Moreover, only Rembrandt used a quartz ground. Pickenoy and Backer employed a double ground commonly found in paintings executed in Amsterdam in the first half of the seventeenth century, which consisted of a red layer covered by a grey/beige layer. Further research is required, but based on what we already know it seems unlikely that even these two artists' priming layers came from the same batch.

It has been argued that the great hall was conceived as a unified sequence of civic guardsmen flowing from one painting to the next. The flight of steps in Backer's painting, for example, leads into Van der Helst's, and the building on the right of Pickenoy's picture continues into Backer's painting [FIG. 60]. A closer look at the locations depicted in the four paintings on the long wall and Van der Helst's painting on the north-west wall reveals that each painter had a different point of departure. While it seems likely that they agreed to, or were instructed to, paint their figures life-size, there was no such agreement in place when it came to the architectural backdrops. As for the steps in Backer's painting running up to Van der Helst's, any illusion that the guardsmen in one of the paintings could step into the other is negated by the position of the steps further back in Backer's painting. Because of their position

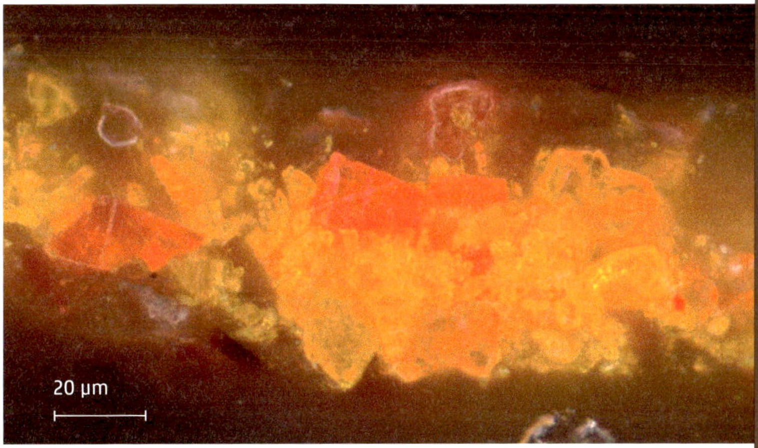


**58**
Paint cross-section taken from Lieutenant Wilhem van Ruytenburch's buff coat showing a mixture of pararealgar and semi-amorphous pararealgar

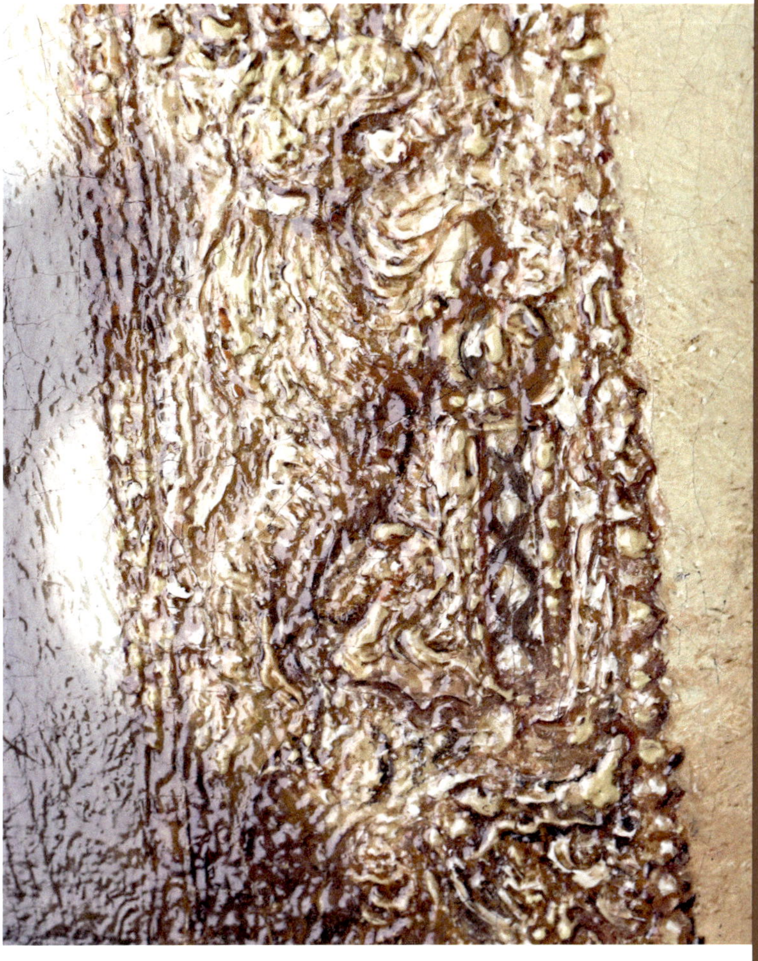

**59**
Detail of Lieutenant Wilhem van Ruytenburch's buff coat in raking light

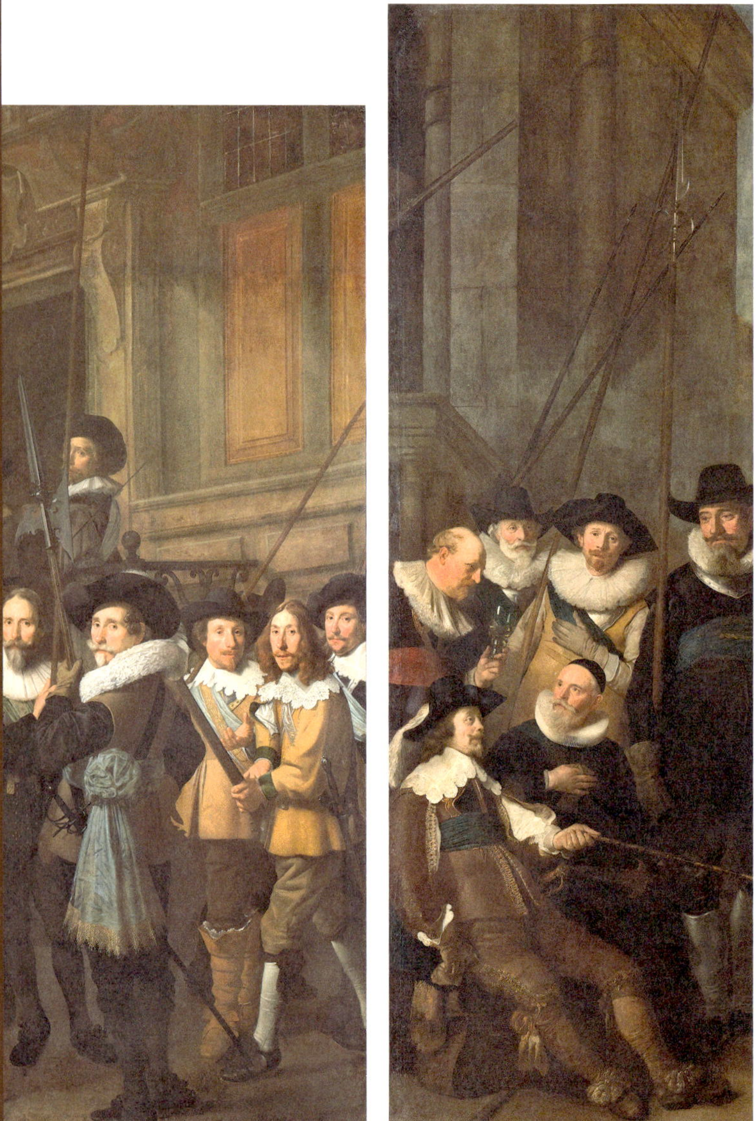

**60**
Detail of the far right side of Pickenoy's painting for the great hall next to a detail of the far left side of Jacob Backer's painting
[FIGS 8, 9]

in space, the figures on those steps had to be less than life-size and the figures in Van der Helst's painting seem therefore to be giants in comparison. Both Van der Helst and Pickenoy chose to include a landmark in their portraits that left no question as to the district that was represented, while the architecture in Backer's and Rembrandt's pictures is purely fictional. Van der Helst arranged the troop in front of the brewery 'The White Rooster' ('De Witte Haan'), which was the gathering place in district 8 of the guardsmen he depicted. This locale is not identifiable by the architecture in the painting, but by the white rooster painted on the barrel on the right. The guardsman straddling this barrel was the brewery's owner. The architecture in Backer's painting has been described as 'Flemish classicism' in the past, but is, at any rate, the product of the painter's imagination [FIG. 9]. The building on the right of Pickenoy's picture is also fanciful [FIG. 8], but the notion that it continues into Backer's portrait is simply incorrect. A close look at the latter reveals a classical porch jutting out from either the front or the back of the depicted structure [FIG. 60]. It is not possible for this porch to have sprouted out of the side of the building in Pickenoy's painting. In the left background of Pickenoy's work we see the no longer extant Jan Roodenpoort tower, which occupied the south-east corner of district IV and served as its clock tower. Pickenoy's guardsmen are assembled at some point along the west side of Singel, one of the major canals in the district. The architectural disunity continues (and would have been especially apparent to contemporary viewers) when we move from Pickenoy's painting to Rembrandt's, where the backdrop, as we have seen, is an imaginary city gate.

It does not seem likely that someone was charged with the task of coordinating the individual civic guard portraits to make a whole. It is clear that the architecture was conceived to give the impression that each painting was set in a different and distinct section of the city, rather than along one and the same street. While the buildings do not in fact flow into one another, the viewer springs from actual locations in the city to purely imaginary ones, and from imaginary ones to ones that are both imaginary and symbolic. The individual districts represented by the portrayed guardsmen were meant to stand out rather than merge into a homogeneous whole.

Van Hoogstraten's critique of the civic guard pieces in which the figures are lined up in 'disgusting rows', with the heads all on the same level, should also be kept in mind. Van Hoogstraten was an apprentice in Rembrandt's workshop in the period when Rembrandt was working on *The Night Watch* or shortly afterwards. The pupil's criticism of Pickenoy's painting was obviously derived from his teacher, who set out in his masterpiece to do the opposite of what that artist was doing in the work that would be hung next to his. Rembrandt was not trying to fit in, but to stand out.

## OPERATION NIGHT WATCH: CONSERVATION TREATMENT

Discovering how the painting was created was, of course, not the only reason for launching the extensive research project Operation Night Watch, nor indeed the most important one. Of primary importance was establishing the condition of the work and evaluating whether or not conservation treatment was necessary. It was determined that, although the condition is not alarming, conservation will substantially increase the aesthetic experience of the picture and contribute significantly to its long-term preservation.

Beginning with the canvas support, there are twelve repaired cuts, nine large mended tears and twelve inserts covering damages. While these require no further handling, there were two issues that necessitated immediate structural treatment. First of all, deformations in the form of bulges had developed in the canvas, especially in the upper left corner. Moreover, the weight of the wax-resin lined canvas had caused the formation of a 'belly' in the lower half of the painting – in other words, the picture was sagging here. These problems were tackled at the beginning of 2022 when the heavy wooden stretcher, to which the painting had been attached in 1976, was replaced with a new, lightweight aluminium strainer using a spring system to ensure an even distribution of tension in the canvas.

There are numerous areas, such as Van Ruytenburch's buff coat, that are in very good condition. Others, however, are in poor condition due to the degradation of the paint and the many past treatments the work has undergone. In places, such as the powder boy's leg, there is pronounced cracking of the paint surface. In others, such as the faces of some of the guardsmen and the dog in the lower right corner of the composition, there is extensive abrasion [FIGS. 61, 63]. In the latter, the ground layer

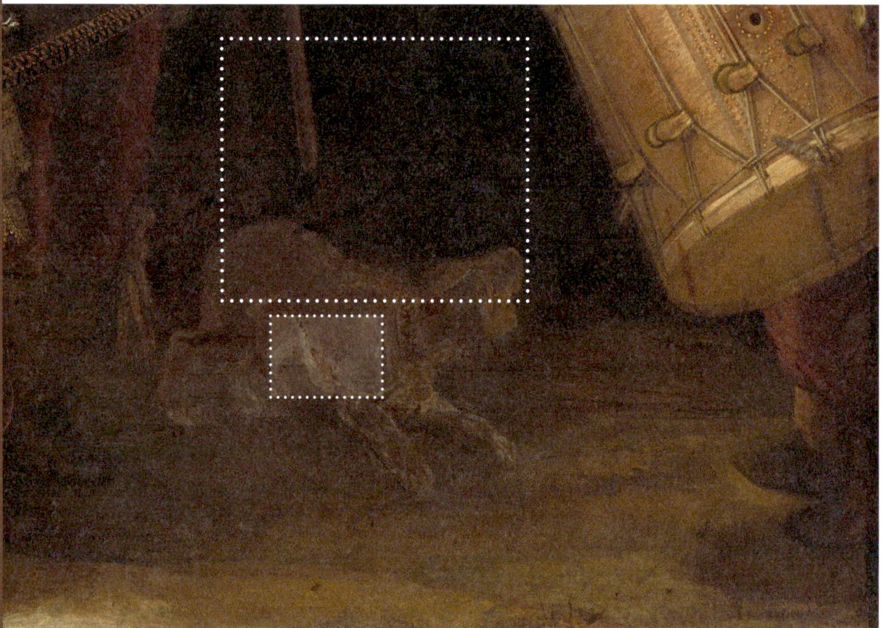

**61**
Detail of the lower right corner of *The Night Watch*

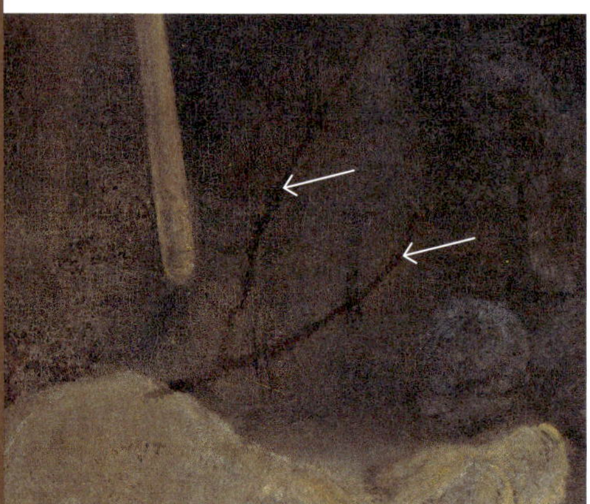

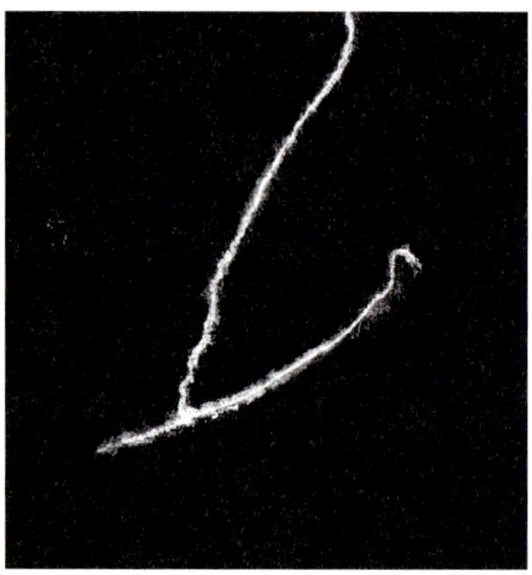

**62**
Detail just above the dog showing the discoloured retouches of the cuts

**63**
Detail of the MA-XRF manganese distribution map, showing umber pigment in the oil paint that was used for restoring cuts in the canvas

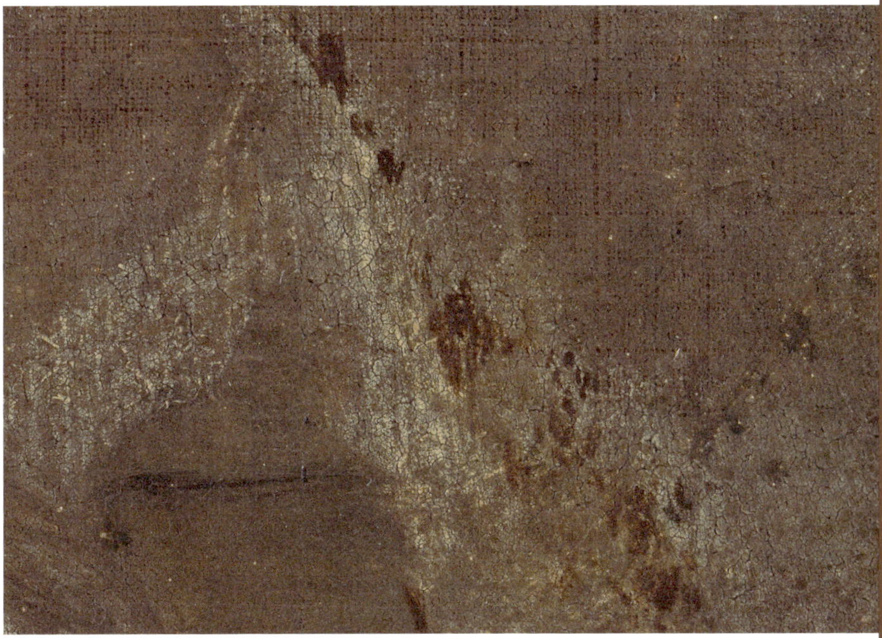

64
Detail of the dog showing abraded areas (see large detail on p. 74)

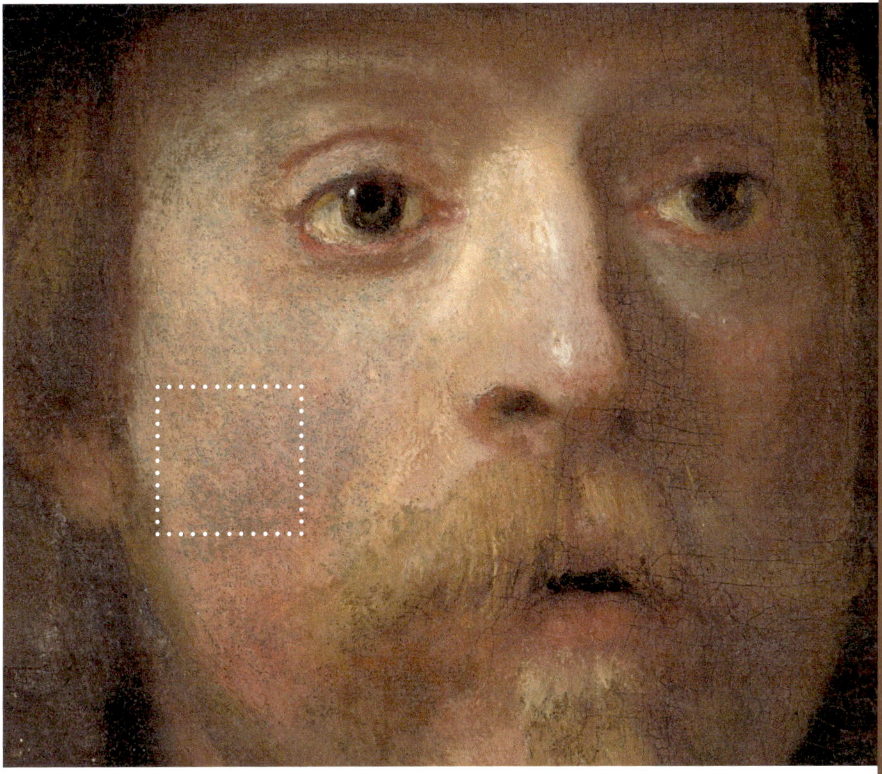

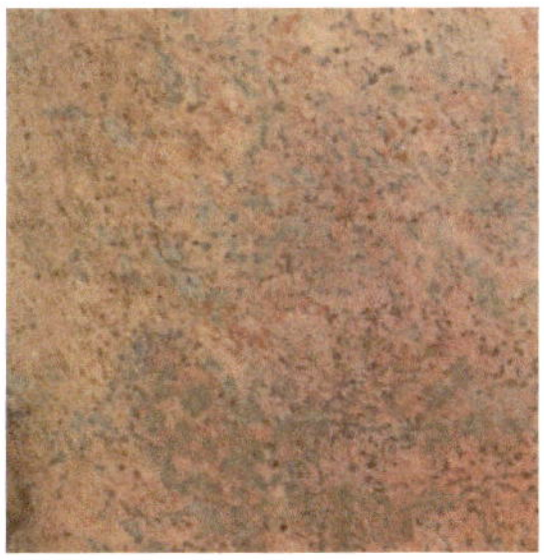

65
From close by, Captain Frans Banninck Cocq appears to have blackheads. These are actually tiny pinpoint losses caused by bits of the leaded oil that originated in the impregnation layer and made their way to the surface of the painting, boring miniscule holes along the way

and even the tops of the canvas threads are exposed. The dark background is severely abraded, as are Captain Banninck Cocq's black doublet and breeches, while the red lake of his socks has faded and is degraded.

It was believed in the past that the brown quartz ground had darkened considerably, to the detriment of the painting's appearance, but recent research has disproved this assumption. During the 1975–1976 campaign (necessitated by the knife attack discussed above), the conservators were afforded very little time and much of the abrasion and small losses throughout were thus left unretouched. This has dramatically affected the overall appearance of the picture. In the areas that were retouched, such as the faces, the twelve cuts, the old inserts and the tears, it often extends over the original paint. In the 1970s, it was customary to use oil paint for retouching, which inevitably darkens over time [FIGS. 62, 63]. Nowadays, synthetic materials that do not discolour and are easier to remove are used.

While the old retouchings can be removed and the damaged areas retouched again, not all of the picture's condition problems can be remedied at this point in time. An example is discoloured smalt, a pigment made of finely ground cobalt blue glass that was employed extensively in *The Night Watch*, often in combination with other pigments. It was used, for example, in the purple clothing of the shooting musketeer. The blue and pink smalt-containing paints of the light side of his doublet are better preserved than those of the side in shadow, which is now a translucent, almost monochrome brown. Another irreversible degradation problem has been caused by lead soap protrusions that have broken through the paint surface resulting in tiny pinpoint paint losses [FIG. 65]. These protrusions were caused by the leaded oil of the impregnation layer and follow the sweeping brushstrokes in the MA-XRF lead map [FIG. 46]. The many treatments in the past as well as fluctuating climate conditions have exacerbated the problem.

One of the greatest questions confronting the Operation Night Watch team is what – if anything – should be done about the fact that the painting is crooked. The imprint of the bars of the original strainer (the wooden frame onto which the canvas was stretched) is apparent in the MA-XRF lead map. These bars are somewhat askew, as are the seams of the canvas [FIG. 44]. These are clear indications that the painting as we now know it is not level, but slants down to the right. In order to correct it, extensions would have to be made and the parts of the image that are missing would have to be reconstructed. Is this a desirable solution?

Finally, a note on the condition of the last material that was applied to the picture, the varnish. Three or four layers of dammar varnish were applied to *The Night Watch* between 1975 and 1990. These have yellowed, but more significantly they have become very dull. Compromising the painting's appearance even more are the remains of varnishes pre-dating 1975.

## CUSTOMER SATISFACTION

*The Night Watch* is the strangest civic guard portrait ever made. As we have seen, it includes many more figures than the eighteen guardsmen who paid to have themselves immortalized, and some of the extras have purely symbolic roles. There are more types of weapons depicted than in any other militia painting of its kind, and some of them were no longer in use at the time it was created. Several guardsmen also wear costumes from a bygone age. The figures are shown in action and the painting is not evenly lit, but veiled in shadow with spotlights illuminating key players. Although the seventeenth-century guidebooks fail to mention it specifically, *The Night Watch* must have struck the original visitors to the great hall of the Kloveniersdoelen as a very unusual work, totally different from the other portraits hanging there, or anywhere else. Probably even more than for present-day viewers, their immediate reaction would have been that they were looking at a history piece, instead of a civic guard portrait.

One wonders whether Captain Frans Banninck Cocq and the other sitters were happy with the way they were portrayed. Based in part on a comment of Samuel van Hoogstraten's that Rembrandt made 'more work of the large image of his choosing, than of the individual likenesses he had been contracted to paint', a now debunked myth that they were dissatisfied arose in the early twentieth century. Certainly, some of the guardsmen who only appear with their faces in the background of the painting may have felt short-changed, but they did pay less than their colleagues who are portrayed prominently in the foreground at full-length. And now that the compositional sketch of the painting has been revealed, it is clear that these sitters knew exactly what to expect.

Captain Banninck Cocq and Lieutenant Wilhem van Ruytenburch, if not the entire troop, must have found the picture very flattering, not because Rembrandt made them look more handsome than they actually were, but because they are seen performing the essential duty of the civic guard. They are marching out to defend the city from its enemies. This was not a real, one-time event, as the old-fashioned clothing, fantasy architecture and purely symbolic figures make clear, but the very function of the Amsterdam civic guard since its founding. Rather than simply being portrayed, the civic guardsmen in *The Night Watch* represent the city's defenders throughout history. One cannot help thinking that Frans Banninck Cocq could have suspected that *The Night Watch* would 'outlive all of its rivals'. And, of course, he would have applauded any effort to ensure his portrait's longevity.

## LITERATURE


Jonathan Bikker and Gwen Tauber, 'Odd Men Out: Govert Flinck and Joachim von Sandrart's Civic Guard Portraits for the Kloveniersdoelen', *Simiolus* 38 (2015–16), no. 4, pp. 260–272

Fréderique Broers, Ige Verslype, Koen W. Bossers, Frederik Vanmeert, Victor Gonzalez, Jan Garrevoet, Annelies van Loon, Esther van Duijn, Anna Krekeler, Nouchka De Keyser, Ilse Steeman, Petria Noble, Koen Janssens, Florian Meier, Katrien Keune, 'Correlated X-ray Fluorescence and Ptychographic Nano-tomography on Rembrandt's *The Night Watch* Reveals Unknown Lead "Layer"', *Science Advances* 9 (2023), no. 50

Jacob Bruyn et al., *A Corpus of Rembrandt Paintings*, vol. 3, The Hague/Boston/London 1989, pp. 430–485, no. A 146

Jessica Carter, Annelies van Loon, Katrien Keune, Emily Froment, 'From Purple to Brown: Using Degradation Products in Reconstructions of a Complex Smalt Paint Mixture in *The Night Watch* to Study Color Change', *Preprints ICOM-CC 20th Triennial Conference Valencia* (2023)

H. Colenbrander, 'De decoratie van de Grote Zaal van de Kloveniersdoelen: een vooropgezet plan?', *Jaarboek Amstelodamum* 105 (2013), pp. 218–237

H. Colenbrander, 'Hoe hoog hing de *Nachtwacht*? Een kwestie van ellen, voeten en duimen', *Jaarboek Amstelodamum* 105 (2013), pp. 238–275

Sebastien A.C. Dudok van Heel, '*The Night Watch* and the Entry of Marie de' Medici. A New Interpretation of the Original Place and Significance of the Painting', *The Rijksmuseum Bulletin* 57 (2009), no. 1, pp. 5–41

Sebastien A.C. Dudok van Heel, 'Frans Banninck Cocq's Troop in Rembrandt's *Night Watch*. The Identification of the Guardsmen', *The Rijksmuseum Bulletin* 57 (2009), no. 1, pp. 43–86

Esther van Duijn, '"Like a drunkard, the diseased painting craved the regenerating alcohol ..." The Numerous Varnish Treatments of Rembrandt's *The Night Watch* between 1889 and 1936', in Esther van Duijn and Petria Noble (eds.), *Rembrandt Conservation Histories*, London/ Amsterdam 2021, pp. 138–151

Esther van Duijn and Jan Piet Filedt Kok, 'The Restorations of Rembrandt's "Night watch"', in Jane Martineau and David Bomford (eds.), *The Art of Conservation*, London 2024, pp. 268–303 (first published in *The Burlington Magazine* 158, February 2016)

Esther van Duijn and Ige Verslype (eds.), *Interim Condition-Research Report, Synopsis*, May–June 2021 (unpublished)

Francesca Gabrieli, John K. Delaney, Robert G. Erdmann, Victor Gonzalez, Annelies van Loon, Patrick Smulders, Roy Berkeveld, Robert van Langh, Katrien Keune, 'Reflectance Imaging Spectroscopy (RIS) for Operation Night Watch: Challenges and Achievements of Imaging Rembrandt's Masterpiece in the Glass Chamber at the Rijksmuseum', *Sensors* 21 (2021), no. 20, p. 6855

Victor Gonzalez, Marine Cotte, Gilles Wallez, Annelies van Loon, Wout de Nolf, Myriam Eveno, Katrien Keune, Petria Noble, Joris Dik, 'Unraveling the Composition of Rembrandt's Impasto through the Identification of Unusual Plumbonacrite by Multimodal X-ray Diffraction Analysis', *Angewandte Chemie International Edition* 58 (2019), no. 17, pp. 5619–5622

Victor Gonzalez, Ida Fazlic, Marine Cotte, Frederik Vanmeert, Arthur Gestels, Steven De Meyer, Fréderique Broers, Joen Hermans, Annelies van Loon, Koen Janssens, Petria Noble, Katrien Keune, 'Lead (II) Formate in Rembrandt's Night Watch: Detection and Distribution from the Macro-to the Micro-scale', *Angewandte Chemie* 62 (2023), no. 16

Karin M. Groen, 'Earth Matters: The Origin of the Material Used for the Preparation of the Night Watch and Many Other Canvases in Rembrandt's Workshop after 1640', *Art Matters* 3 (2005), pp. 138–154

Egbert Haverkamp-Begemann, *Rembrandt: The Nightwatch*, Princeton (NJ) 1982

Nouchka De Keyser, Fréderique Broers, Frederik Vanmeert, Annelies van Loon, Francesca Gabrieli, Steven De Meyer, Arthur Gestels, Victor Gonzalez, Erma Hermens, Petria Noble, Florian Meier, Koen Janssens, Katrien Keune, 'Discovery of Pararealgar and Semiamorphous Pararealgar in Rembrandt's *The Night Watch*: Analytical Study and Historical Contextualization', *Heritage Science* 12 (2024), art. no. 237

B. Kist, 'Een curieus militair tafereel', *De Kroniek van het Rembrandthuis* 40 (1988), no. 1, pp. 1–23

Paul Knevel, *Burgers in het geweer. De schutterijen van Holland, 1550–1700*, Hilversum 1994

Marijke Kok, 'Rembrandts *Nachtwacht*. Van Feeststoet tot Schuttersstuk', *Bulletin van het Rijksmuseum* 15 (1967), no. 4, pp. 116–121

Annelies van Loon, Petria Noble, Anna Krekeler, Geert Van der Snickt, Koen Janssens, Yoshinari Abe, Izumi Nakai, Joris Dik, 'Artificial Orpiment, a New Pigment in Rembrandt's Palette', *Heritage Science* 5 (2017), art. no. 26

Wilhelm Martin, *Van Nachtwacht tot feeststoet. Lotgevallen, inhoud en betekenis van Rembrandt's schuttersstuk in het Rijksmuseum te Amsterdam*, Amsterdam 1947

Norbert E. Middelkoop, '"Met schuttersschilderijen behangen": de Amsterdamse schuttersstukken in de drie doelens', *Jaarboek Amstelodamum* 105 (2013), pp. 12–107

Pieter Scheltema, 'De schilderijen in de drie doelens te Amsterdam, beschreven door G. Schaep, 1653', *Aemstels Oudheid* 7 (1885), pp. 1–141, esp. pp. 135–139

Gary Schwartz, *The Night Watch*, Amsterdam 2008

J. Six, 'Een teekening van Bartholomeus van der Helst', *Oud Holland* 27 (1909), pp. 142–148

Derk P. Snoep, *Praal en propaganda. Triumfalia in de Noordelijke Nederlanden in de 16de en 17de eeuw*, Utrecht 1974, pp. 39–76

Christian Tümpel, 'Beobachtungen zur "Nachtwache"', in Otto von Simson and Jan Kelch (eds.), *Neue Beiträge zur Rembrandt-Forschung*, Berlin 1973, pp. 162–175

Christian Tümpel, 'De Amsterdamse schuttersstukken', in Marijke Carasso-Kok and J. Levy-van Halm (eds.), *Schutters in Holland. Kracht en zenuwen van de stad*, Zwolle 1988, pp. 74–103

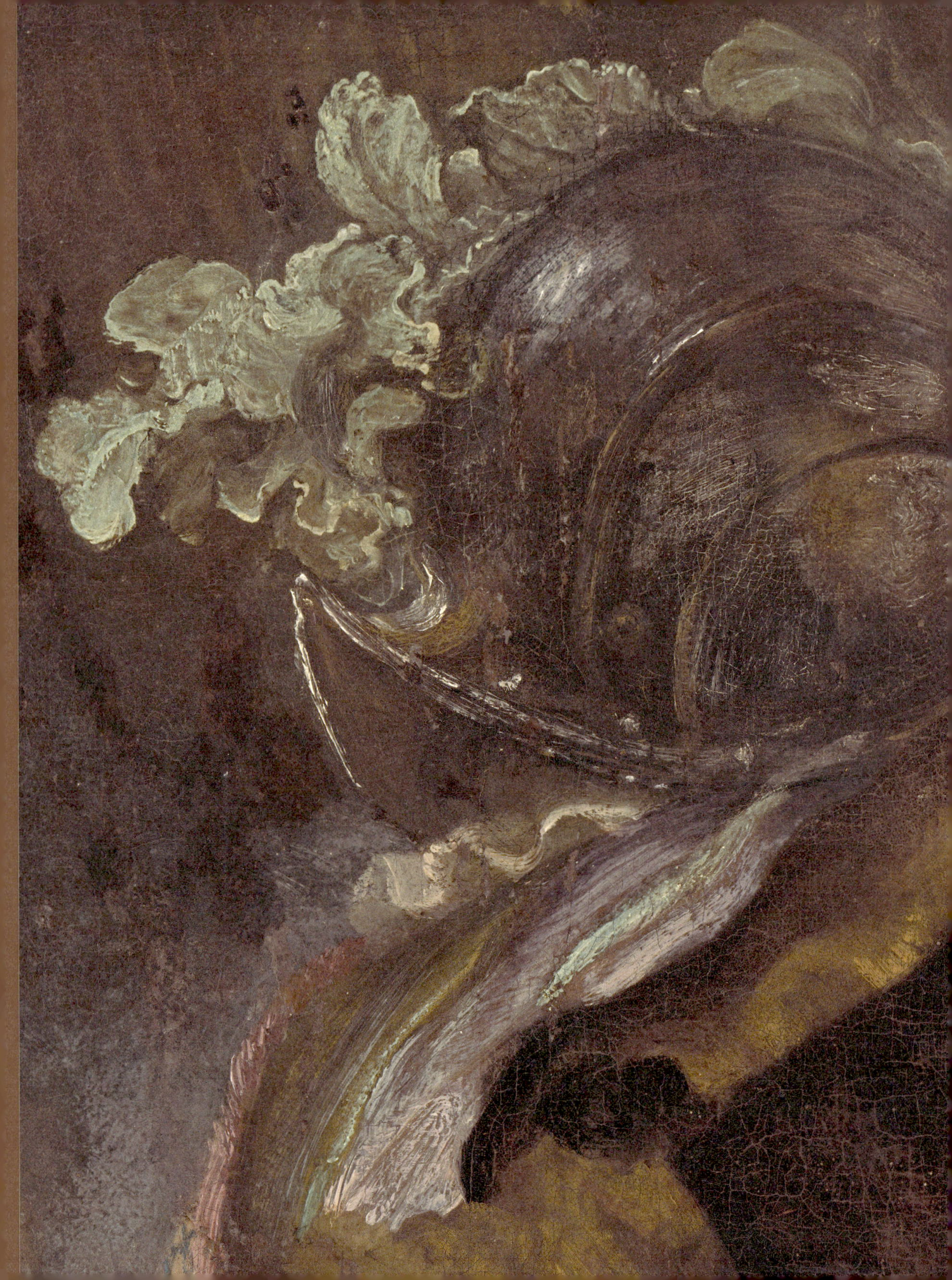

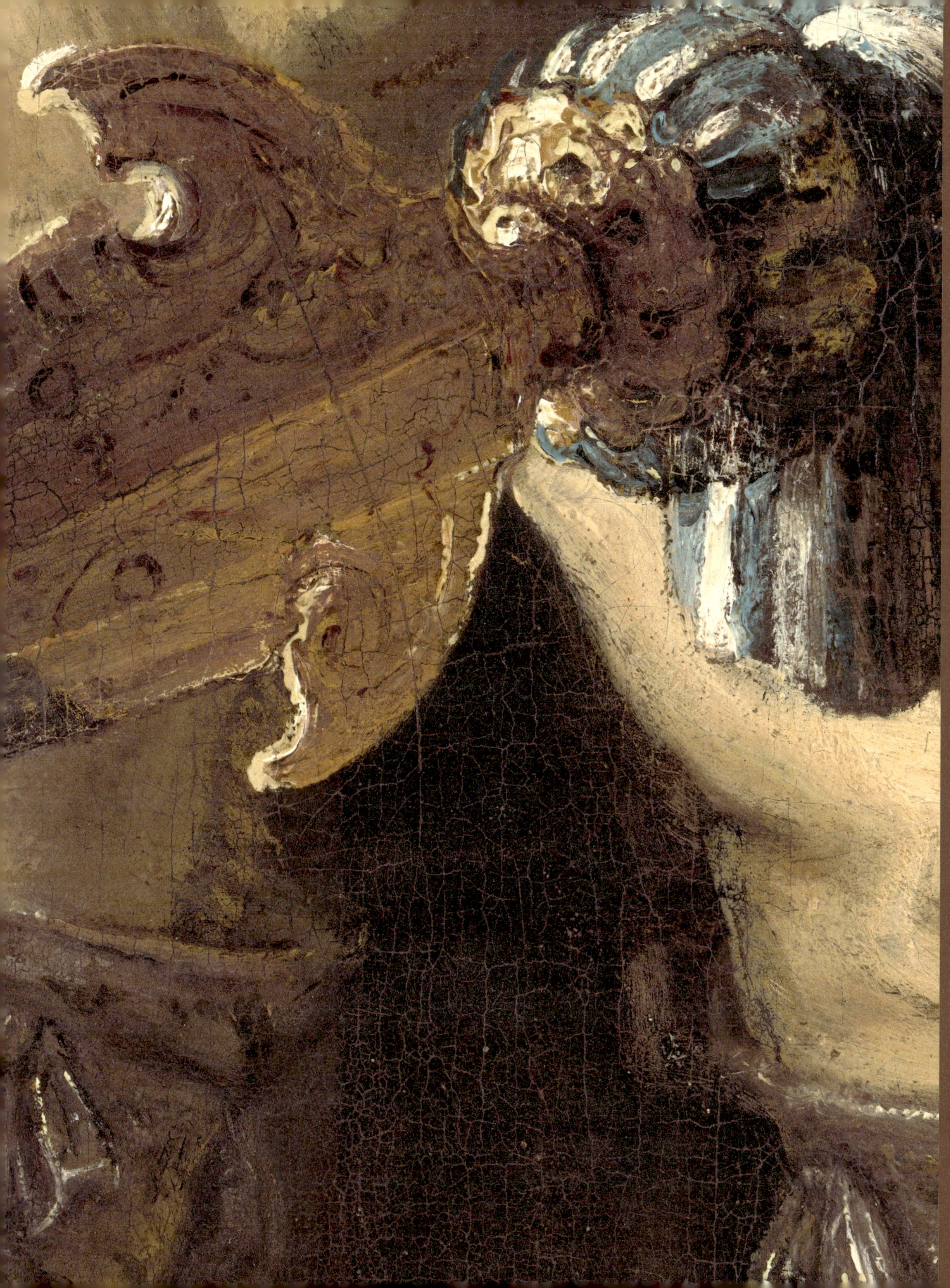

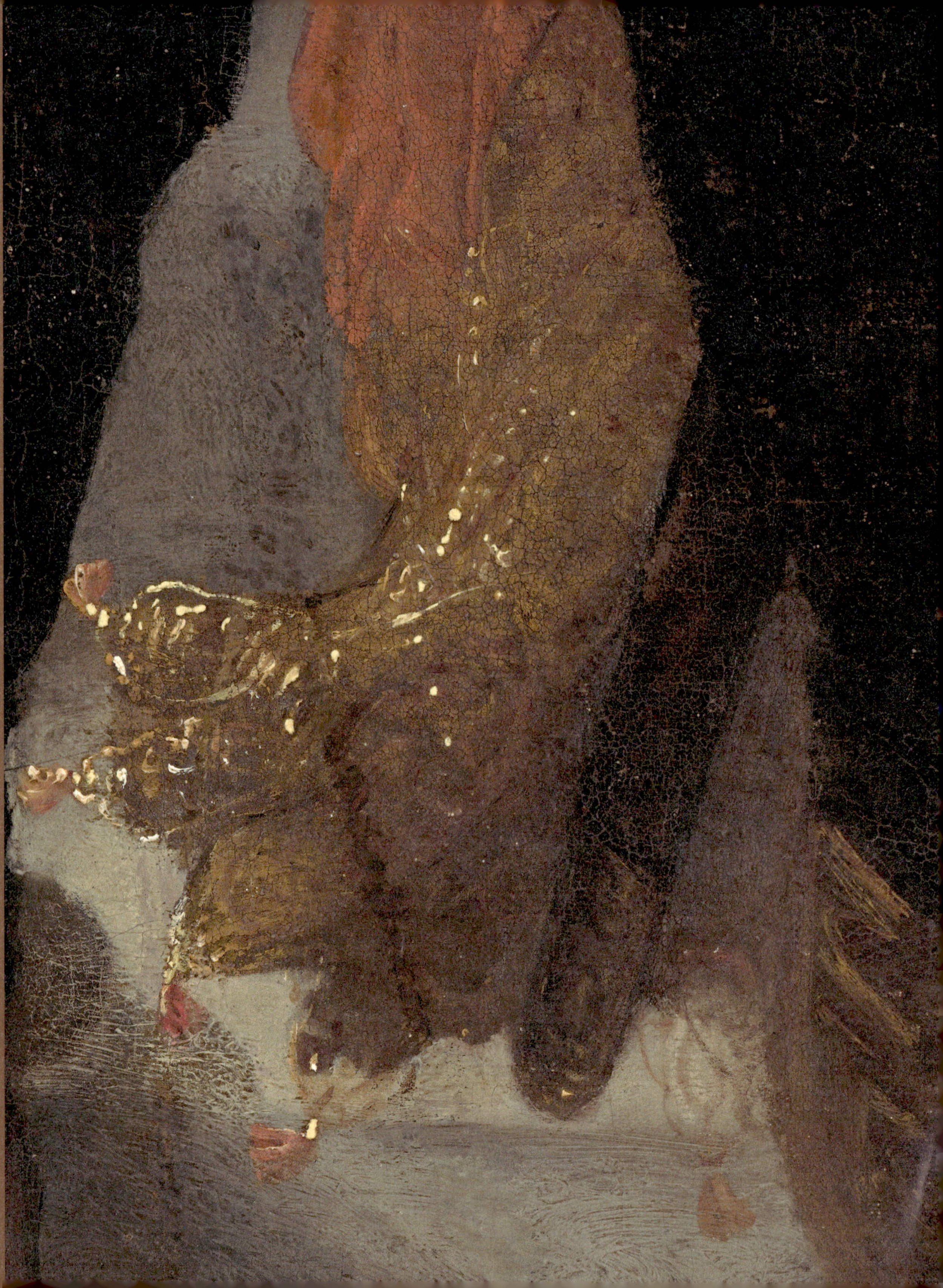

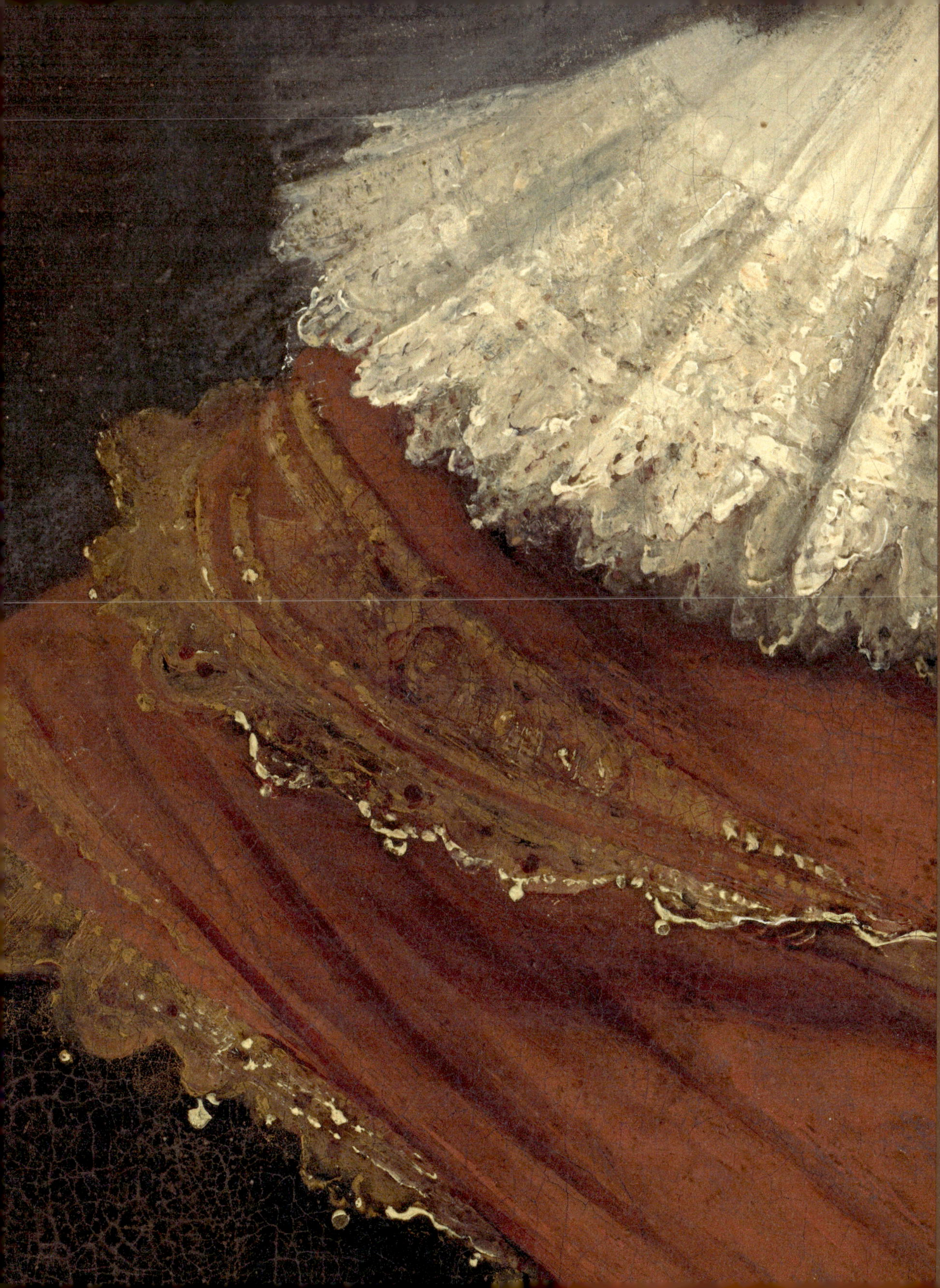

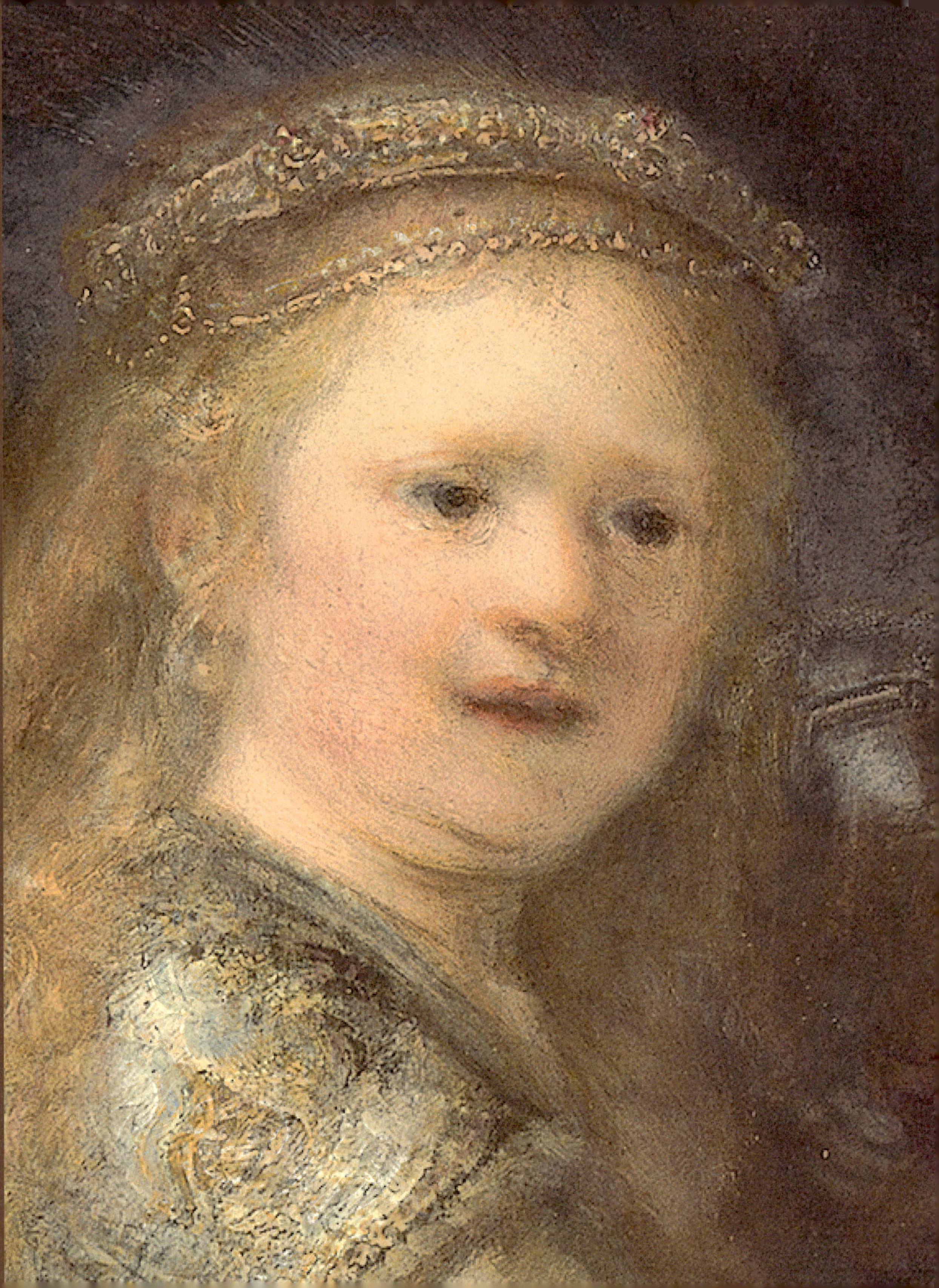